Implications of Remote Working Adoption on Place Based Policies

A FOCUS ON G7 COUNTRIES

This document, as well as any data and map included herein, are without prejudice to the status of or sovereignty over any territory, to the delimitation of international frontiers and boundaries and to the name of any territory, city or area.

The statistical data for Israel are supplied by and under the responsibility of the relevant Israeli authorities. The use of such data by the OECD is without prejudice to the status of the Golan Heights, East Jerusalem and Israeli settlements in the West Bank under the terms of international law.

Note by Turkey
The information in this document with reference to "Cyprus" relates to the southern part of the Island. There is no single authority representing both Turkish and Greek Cypriot people on the Island. Turkey recognises the Turkish Republic of Northern Cyprus (TRNC). Until a lasting and equitable solution is found within the context of the United Nations, Turkey shall preserve its position concerning the "Cyprus issue".

Note by all the European Union Member States of the OECD and the European Union
The Republic of Cyprus is recognised by all members of the United Nations with the exception of Turkey. The information in this document relates to the area under the effective control of the Government of the Republic of Cyprus.

Please cite this publication as:
OECD (2021), *Implications of Remote Working Adoption on Place Based Policies: A Focus on G7 Countries*, OECD Publishing, Paris, *https://doi.org/10.1787/b12f6b85-en*.

ISBN 978-92-64-46647-0 (print)
ISBN 978-92-64-93065-0 (pdf)

Photo credits: Cover © dennisvdw/Getty images

Corrigenda to publications may be found on line at: *www.oecd.org/about/publishing/corrigenda.htm*.

Foreword

COVID-19 has accelerated the digitalisation of working and social interactions. Global lockdowns to contain the pandemic have forced firms and workers to perform a wide range of daily functions through virtual means, and, in turn, have accelerated the uptake and acceptance of remote working, which will likely remain in its hybrid form after the pandemic.

Remote working has already revealed a number of benefits to our lives including reduced transport-related greenhouse gas emissions, greater flexibility of working and potential cost savings for firms. Yet, not everybody has been able to benefit from the virtual forms of interaction due to gaps in digital infrastructure and digital skills across places, workers and firms. Since a hybrid form of remote working is likely to be one of the lasting legacies of the pandemic, and potentially further accelerated by technological progress and investments, governments need to facilitate and enable this transition.

Remote working opens up new opportunities for regions outside large cities to attract new residents, boost economic activities and revitalise communities. In recent decades, rural regions have faced lower growth in living standards and higher population decline and ageing than cities. Attracting new workers and firms that embrace remote working offers rural regions the possibility to mitigate or reverse these trends. People with the potential to work remotely could be attracted to relocate to regions outside large cities offering affordable and suitable housing, lower costs of living and better access to environmental amenities. Firms paying high-location costs in cities could also find it profitable to change their real estate strategy either by downscaling or by relocating part or indeed all of their headquarters.

Despite these opportunities for rural regions, a big exodus from cities is not envisioned. Cities have historically attracted the bulk of workers and firms due to the benefits associated with economies of agglomeration. These benefits are likely to continue to shape firms' location strategies, including the importance of access to skilled workers, customers, networks and suppliers, even as cities continue to reinvent themselves. While a mass exodus remains unlikely, national policies will need to ensure that regional competition to attract workers and firms does not lead to worse overall outcomes, especially over the longer term.

This report proposes a number of policy takeaways to guide short- and long-term policy making to better prepare regions for what may be a 'new normal'. The report relies on real-time subnational data and national statistical surveys to analyse changes in people's mobility patterns and the determinants of remote working adoption across types of workers and places. The report also identifies different scenarios of settlement patterns that could emerge post-COVID-19, highlighting how changing patterns of work could have an impact on regional development and a range of policy areas, including infrastructure, healthcare and the environment.

Irrespective of the post-pandemic scenario and future changes driven by technology, policies need to be forward-looking and proactive to seize the potential benefits of remote working. National and subnational governments can play a decisive role in supporting the right conditions for workers and firms aiming to adopt remote working, whether hybrid or full-time, while improving people's quality of life in all types of regions.

Acknowledgements

This publication was produced by the OECD Centre for Entrepreneurship, SMEs, Regions and Cities (CFE), led by Lamia Kamal-Chaoui, Director, as part of the programme of work of the Regional Development Policy Committee (RDPC).

The report was prepared with support of the Ministry of Land, Infrastructure, Transport and Tourism of Japan. Special thanks are due to Arisa Osawa and Taku Onodera from the National Spatial Planning and Regional Policy Bureau of the Ministry for their support throughout the process. The OECD is grateful to country delegates to the OECD Regional Development Policy Committee who coordinated comments and responses to a policy survey for this report. They include Isis Bozzano-Bae from Canada, Luc Faradi from France, Till Spannagel from Germany and Sabrina Lucatelli, Crescenzo Rajola and Flavia Terribile and from Italy.

The OECD team elaborating the report included Enrique Garcilazo, project coordinator, Head of the Regional and Rural Policy Unit in the Regional Development and Multilevel Governance Division, led by Dorothée Allain-Dupré. The report was drafted by Ana Moreno Monroy (Chapter 1), Michelle Marshalian (Chapter 2), Cem Özgüzel (Chapter 3), Andres Sanabria and Fernando Riaza (Chapter 4) with contributions from Miguel Carlos Manjon (Rovira I Virgili University, Spain) (Chapter 1 and 2) and the support of Maria Paula Caldas and Kana Murail. Nadim Ahmad, Deputy Director of CFE and Alain Dupeyras, former director of the Regional Development and Multilevel Governance Division provided guidance throughout the report.

Special thanks are due to other CFE colleagues who provided inputs and feedback to the report. They include Mael Astruc-Le Souder, David Burgalassi, Mattia Corbetta, Alexander Lembcke, Tadashi Matsumoto, Andrew Paterson, Tetsuji Sugayoshi, Paolo Veneri, and Wessel Vermeulen. Thanks also to Claire Hoffmann for statistical support.

The report was submitted to delegates of the Working Party on Rural Policy for information and approval at its 25th session that took place on 3-4 May 2021 under the code [CFE/RDPC/RUR (2021)/1]. The final version was edited by Andrew Brenner, and Pilar Philip led the formatting process and prepared the manuscript for publication.

Table of contents

Tables

Figures

Boxes

Follow OECD Publications on:

http://twitter.com/OECD_Pubs

http://www.facebook.com/OECDPublications

http://www.linkedin.com/groups/OECD-Publications-4645871

http://www.youtube.com/oecdilibrary

http://www.oecd.org/oecddirect/

This book has...

StatLinks

A service that delivers Excel® files from the printed page!

Look for the *StatLinks* at the bottom of the tables or graphs in this book. To download the matching Excel® spreadsheet, just type the link into your Internet browser, starting with the ***https://doi.org*** prefix, or click on the link from the e-book edition.

Executive Summary

The Covid-19 crisis has brought substantial changes to the way people interact, and firms conduct their business. Faced with containment measures, many workers have needed to adapt to remote working, while firms were also forced to quickly shift activities onto virtual platforms through online services and online ordering, which led to a significant acceleration in the up-take of digitalisation. Although the capacity to adapt is unequal across regions, with large cities hosting the largest share of tele-workable jobs, increasing digitalisation presents new opportunities and indeed challenges, including where workers live and firms locate.

Historically, cities have attracted most workers and firms due to economies of agglomeration. A greater adoption of remote working could incentivise the demand for places outside large cities that can offer affordable and suitable housing and office spaces with better access to environmental amenities. Many of these locations however will likely be located within close proximity to cities, which will remain important hubs of opportunity.

In many countries, these transitions have already begun to emerge but the extent to which they will be long-lasting remains uncertain, not least as the pandemic is far from over. Notwithstanding those uncertainties, this report considers the potential future effects on places of remote working adoption, and proposes a way forward to help all regions seize the opportunities this phenomenon presents.

The report relies on real-time data at subnational levels and national labour force surveys to analyse changes in people's mobility patterns and the determinants of remote working adoption across types of workers and places. The analysis covers a period from the beginning of the COVID-19 crisis in 2020 until early 2021 (in the midst of the third COVID-19 wave in many countries). The report also takes stock of policy responses to the increasing prevalence of remote working adoption from a survey undertaken in G7 countries, from which broader lessons are drawn for all OECD economies.

The first chapter outlines people's mobility patterns from home to work at subnational levels, relying on new sources of real-time data based on mobile phone activity. The second chapter explores the socio-economic determinants of remote working across regions, based on national level labour force statistics as well as microdata on broadband speeds. The third sheds light on the uneven effects of remote working adoption on the labour market, particularly employment and wages in different types of areas. Finally, the fourth chapter sets out the possible effects of COVID-19 on the spatial distribution of people and firms, and outlines current and required policy responses to benefit from the rise in remote working.

The report identifies a number of findings and policy takeaways to guide short- and long-term policy making to better prepare regions for what may be a 'new normal'.

Findings and policy takeaways

From the pandemic

- Throughout 2020 and early 2021 the COVID-19 pandemic had a sustained impact on people's mobility, with some relief during the summer months. The greatest reduction in mobility was seen in regions with large cities (that had the highest levels of mobility to start with), both during the first and second waves, reflecting, in large part, reduced work-related mobility.
- Whilst differences exist in the types of jobs that are amenable to remote working across regions (with higher shares in cities), a critical enabling factor to remote working is good telecommunications infrastructure, which is typically lower in non-metropolitan regions (in terms of coverage and speed).
- While women are more likely to have jobs that could benefit from remote working, female labour force participation rates tend to be lower in non-metropolitan regions, in large part because of the types of activities performed.
- Because high shares of occupations are ill-suited to remote working (or indeed can be replaced by automation) are lower-skilled, the adverse labour market effects of the pandemic were particularly strong for already disadvantaged groups of workers (e.g. young, old, low-skilled and migrants). Some of these groups, particularly old and low-skilled groups, are typically overrepresented outside metropolitan regions.

Looking towards the post-pandemic world

Increased remote working is likely to be a lasting legacy of the crisis. Although the transition towards virtual working was a forced experiment for many, it has produced a number of positive results including the temporary reduction of greenhouse gas emissions, greater potential for improved work-life balance and cost savings. Remote working may also create new job opportunities for people who would not have otherwise joined the labour market, particularly women and people with certain disabilities. These positive aspects, and evidence that remote working can be effective, are likely to mean that remote working arrangements, at least in a hybrid form, are here to stay.

But the transition will require support. Despite the many positive aspects of remote working, the transition will require careful management by governments, firms and indeed workers. The pandemic has also revealed a number of challenges related, for example, to gaps in digital infrastructure, digital skills and differences in the ability of some workers and firms to adopt remote working. These challenges risk increasing the digital divides, especially for smaller firms, the low-skilled, and regions with poor digital infrastructure. In addition, it has also generated, for many, negative social side-effects such as isolation or hidden overtime (some are partly associated with the effects of measurements taken to slow the spread of the virus).

The possibility to work remotely opens up new opportunities for places outside large cities to reach new markets and attract new residents and firms. Greater adoption of virtual working methods and social interactions offer incentives for some workers to relocate outside large cities (either partially or full time). The possibility to work virtually—coupled with a greater availability of suitable housing, lower costs of living and greater environmental amenities outside large cities—can attract workers. For firms, the pandemic has increased the number of companies considering a change in their real estate strategy, either by downscaling or relocating part of the office space. For example, a recent survey of the Japanese government revealed that 14% of companies with headquarters in Tokyo considered changing their real estate strategy as a result of the pandemic. Most of those firms expect to downscale their office space (48%), while the rest expect to relocate part (17%) or their entire (35%) office.

Yet a big exodus from cities is not envisioned as these places are reinventing themselves. Large cities may continue to concentrate most of the skilled workers and firms through ongoing policies to transform themselves and improve quality of life (e.g. 15 minutes cities). For example, a temporary or full relocation of a number of high-skilled workers outside large cities and changes in real estate strategies of firms could ease housing availability for low-skilled workers or promote reconversion of buildings into green areas in some areas of the city. As both metropolitan and non-metropolitan regions are conducting strategies to become more attractive for remote workers, greater regional competition based on temporary measures could result, if it is poorly managed or co-ordinated, in a "race to the bottom" scenario.

Various settlement patterns could emerge in the post-COVID-19 normality due to the increased adoption of remote working. They include: i) structural changes from a permanent movement of high skilled workers outside city centres, ii) expansion of commuting zones around cities as a doughnut effect, iii) intermediate cities becoming increasingly attractive, and iv) business as usual but with greater adoption of remote working. These scenarios might not occur in mutually exclusive forms and will differ across countries and places. Regardless of how the post-pandemic world eventually unfolds, technology will continue to disrupt the benefits of physical proximity and the way people and firms interact. Emerging technologies coupled with a greater adoption of remote working will likely bring new forms of commuting with longer and less frequent commutes for a share of the workforce, which might have environmental and income effects.

Irrespective of the post-pandemic scenario, policies need to be forward-looking and proactive to seize the potential benefits that remote working and other technologies can bring about. Ultimately, people's and business' decisions to relocate, full time or partially, will involve a cost-benefit analysis in which national and subnational government actions can play a decisive role. Changing patterns of work have implications for regional development and a range of policy areas, including infrastructure, business support, healthcare and the environment. Therefore, governments at national and subnational levels should support the right conditions for those workers and firms aiming to adopt hybrid remote working, while improving people's quality of life in all regions. To this end, policy responses from different levels of government should focus on three main areas:

I. Reduce digital divides and facilitate the adoption of remote working across regions, workers and firms by:

- **Making high quality communication services accessible and affordable in all regions.** This involves implementing holistic policies to foster competition in telecommunication markets, simplifying procedures for broadband deployment and creating funding methods to increase connectivity (e.g. demand aggregation models, public-private partnerships, public funding to expand connectivity, coverage obligation in spectrum auctions, bottom-up approaches, and addressing the last mile).
- **Investing in digital skills for workers and ICT capacity for firms, especially SMEs**. This includes implementing training on basic use of ICT technologies and computing, and capacity building on software and ICT maintenance in rural economies.
- **Helping overcome cultural and legal barriers for remote working.** This includes promoting a 'right to telework' and to 'disconnect', conduct information campaigns and guidelines to best deal with remote working, and adapting tax regimes and regulatory frameworks to conduct virtual activities.

II. Improve the attractiveness and accessibility to quality services particularly in non-metropolitan regions by:

- **Adapting support services to enhance conditions for remote working to all population groups, particularly women and youth**. Regardless of the extent to which remote working is adopted, policies to ensuring adequate provision of key support services, such as childcare or work-life balance measures will continue to be important. The COVID-19 crisis also revealed the relevance of physical interactions. Governments can help through support for co-working spaces that can offer network opportunities and quality work conditions for those lacking them. A focus on policies to support older workers and women's labour market participation (either virtually or physically) is relevant to revitalise non-metropolitan regions.

- **Enhancing the provision of quality education and health** outside large cities by addressing gaps in provision that lower the attractiveness of some non-metropolitan regions. Whilst a potential increase in population and thus demand for services can ease the challenges of small-scale provision in non-metropolitan regions, there are a number of direct actions that should be taken to improve quality of education and health, regardless of the future scenario of remote working adoption. These include:
    - regarding education: developing school clusters or networks in which schools formally co-operate under a single leadership to allocate resources more flexibly and efficiently. This could be further supported through more flexible approaches to considering class sizes and other relevant regulations.
    - regarding health: providing incentives for the establishment of multi-disciplinary health centres and reinforcing primary and integrated care provision (which is generally the first contact point for the majority of patients' needs outside large cities). Policies to attract, retain and empower health workers should also be bolstered.
- **Adapting the provision of services to population changes** resulting from greater adoption of remote working.
- **Promoting a greater use of digitalisation to provide services** in all regions (e.g. online education and health). This includes enhancing cooperation with information and telecommunications firms (e.g. real time and big data) to improve the efficiency in the provision of local services.
- **Co-ordinating regional attraction policies**, while discouraging regional strategies to attract economic actors based on tax incentives and subsidies. Place-based policies to boost regional attractiveness should focus on improving quality of life (e.g. transport networks and affordable housing) and business environment (e.g. quality and affordable ICT infrastructure, skills, entrepreneurship and quality governance and regulation).

III. Ensure the outcomes from remote working are efficient and environmentally sustainable by:

- **Developing policies on land use, housing and transportation that are forward-looking and co-ordinated appropriately**. Policies should adapt to different forms of commuting and working styles after COVID-19 (including permanent relocation or dual residency). For example, authorities should ensure that public transport projects are aligned with new co-working and housing projects in non-metropolitan regions, particularly in areas close to large cites.
- **Adapting environmental policies to the effects of a greater dispersion of economic actors.** This includes adjusting energy efficiency policies in housing and resource management (water and waste) to changes in population, while avoiding urban sprawl effects and adapting public transport to new forms of commuting.

1 Effects of COVID-19 on geographic mobility and working habits

This chapter analyses the impact COVID-19 in daily mobility of people across different types of regions. To this end, the chapter uses two new sources of real-time data at the subnational level: Google-maps lifestyle data for TL2 regions in G7 countries data broken down by different types of mobility (e.g. consumer vs workplace), and Mapbox movement data for United States counties and German TL3 regions. The analysis also matches TL2 information with regional data to assess the relationship between mobility trends during February 2020 and February 2021 and regional characteristics.

How much has COVID-19 affected the daily mobility of people, especially in relation to their home-work movements? Has the impact of COVID-19 on mobility been larger in cities than in other areas? Answering these questions requires real-time data that are usually not available from official sources. Recently, non-standard sources of data have been used to analyse the impact of COVID-19 on socio-economic indicators, including mobile-phone, credit card transaction and private business data (Chetty et al., 2020[1]), and mobility reports from Google at the country level (Pareliussen and Glocker, 2021[2]).

This chapter tries to answer these questions by using two new sources of real-time data at the subnational level: Google-maps lifestyle data for TL2 regions in G7 countries data broken down by different types of mobility (e.g. consumer vs workplace) (Google LLC, 2021[3]), and Mapbox movement data for United States counties and German TL3 regions (Mapbox, 2021[4]). The analysis also matches TL2 information with regional data including GDP per capita, the share of urban population and the degree of teleworkability to assess the relationship between mobility trends during February 2020 and February 2021 and regional characteristics.

After this introduction, the next section presents the methodology and results using Google's mobility report data for G7 countries and its relation to regional characteristics. The third section presents the method and results for mobility trends using Mapbox data for Germany and the US. The last section concludes.

Mobility trends and patterns using Google mobility data

This section analyses developments in people's mobility in TL2 regions of Canada, England (UK), France Japan and the US during the period between the 15 February 2020 and the 11 February 2021 using daily data from the Global Mobility Report of Google[1] (Google LLC, 2021[3]). The section starts by describing briefly the processing of Google's data, it then discusses national-level patterns and then proceeds with the analysis of mobility trends for TL2 regions of G7 countries.

Data sources and processing

People's mobility is measured by Google using number of visitors to a set of categorised places, namely:

- "Retail and Recreation" refers to mobility for places like restaurants, cafes, shopping centres, theme parks, museums, libraries, and movie theatres;
- "Grocery and Pharmacy" refers to places like grocery markets, food warehouses, farmers markets, specialty food shops, drug stores, and pharmacies,
- "Transit Stations" refers to places like public transport hubs such as subway, bus, and train stations; and,
- "Workplaces" refers to places of work.[2]

These data are used to compute the percentage change in people's mobility within the geographic area of the considered TL2 region with respect to the median value for the corresponding day of the week of 3 January 2020 to 3 February 2020 period (baseline period).[3] Two time-plots constructed on the basis of this data inform on new trends and/or changes in existing trends in mobility over the period February – February 2021. The next section analyses changes in mobility in each country and fortnight and the following section shows the daily changes in mobility in each TL2 region, both with respect to the areas of:

- "Retail and Recreation" and "Grocery and Pharmacy", indicative of the mobility of consumers, and
- "Transit Stations" and "Workplaces", indicative of the mobility of workers.

For illustrative purposes, the daily time-plots include the name of the leading, median and lower region of each country in each considered place in the last day reported (15 February 2021).

Leaving aside seasonality effects and sample selection biases, reported values around zero would indicate "return to normality" (e.g., within the ±10% interval), whereas large negative and positive values (e.g., above the ±10% interval) would indicate "below normality" and "above normality" situations, respectively.

The mobility time-plots are complemented with the daily change in the "Stringency Index" constructed by (Hale, T., S. Webster, A. Petherick, T. Phillips, and B. Kira, 2020a[5]) to proxy for the strictness of the "lockdown style" policies that (primarily) restrict people's behaviour for the countries of interest.[4] The reported "Stringency Index" of the Oxford Covid-19 Government Response Tracker is the average of indicators on containment and closure policies, such as school closures and restrictions in movement.

Overall mobility trends in G7 countries

Figures Figure 1.1. to Figure 1.7 illustrate how mobility in the G7 countries (by fortnight) changed during the considered period. Three large sub-periods can be distinguished:

- Across countries, there is an initial drop in mobility up until the month of April 2020 (May 2020 in Japan). The magnitude of this initial drop, however, varies between the lowest 40%-50% in Japan (Figure 1.6) and the US (Figure 1.7), up to the 80% in France (Figure 1.3), Italy (Figure 1.5) and England (UK) (Figure 1.2). The impact was particularly severe in retail and recreation places and transit stations.
- There is a subsequent and progressive recovery in the following five months. The "return to normal" (i.e., values within the ±10% interval) happened during summer, although mostly in consumers' mobility, since all countries still showed values below -20% in mobility around public transport hubs and/or workplaces. Only Japan reached "normal values" in all the considered places at the end of September (Figure 1.6).
- The final period shows another soft and continuous decline in mobility, with minimum values around the Christmas period (Germany at the end of December (Figure 1.4); Canada (Figure 1.1) and England (UK) (Figure 1.2) at the beginning of January), with the exception of France (Figure 1.3) and Italy to a lesser extent (early November) (Figure 1.5) and the US (early February) (Figure 1.7). In terms of magnitude and with the exception of Germany, the impact was not as severe as the initial one in April, but it was still substantial (around 20%-30% in Japan (Figure 1.6) and the US (Figure 1.7), but 40%-50% in the rest of the G7 countries). This, however, does not apply to the mobility around grocery stores and pharmacies ("Grocery and Pharmacy" category), which reached "normal values" in all countries.

The most recent data for 2021 indicates a certain stability and slight upturn in mobility that, nevertheless, still remains on average below "normality levels" in an order of magnitude of between 20% (e.g., Japan) and 40% (e.g., Germany and England (UK)). Again, this does not apply to the mobility around grocery stores and pharmacies places which, with the exception of England (UK), remains in "normal values".

Figure 1.1. Mobility in G7 countries and strictness of lockdown policies, Canada

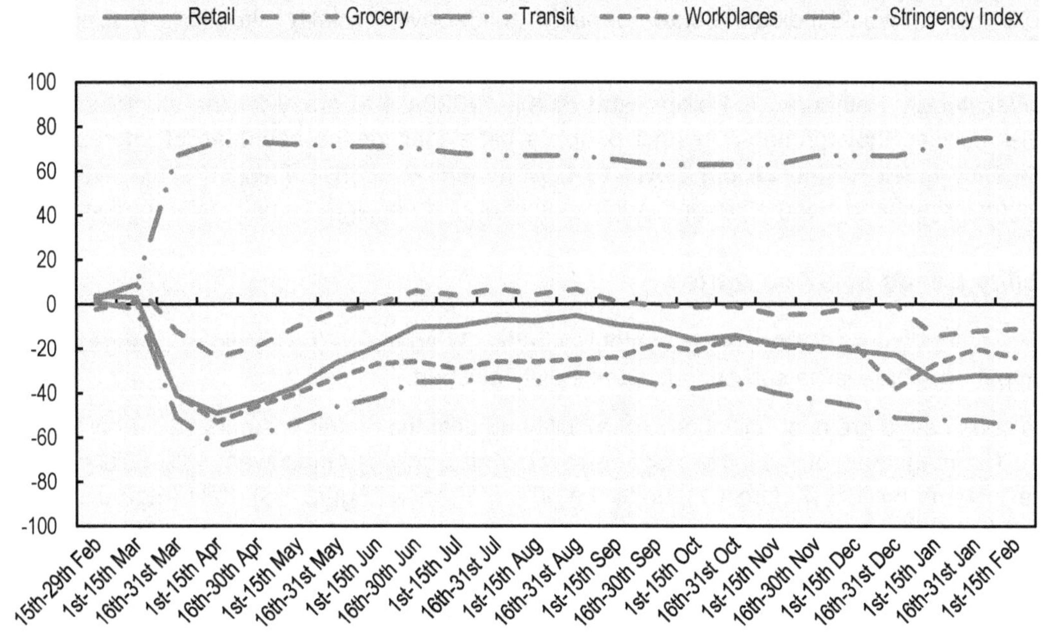

Note: See Figure 1.7 notes.
Source: Authors' elaboration based on (Google LLC, 2021[3]) and (Hale, T., S. Webster, A. Petherick, T. Phillips, and B. Kira, 2020a[5]).

StatLink https://doi.org/10.1787/888934248141

Figure 1.2. Mobility in G7 countries and strictness of lockdown policies, England (UK)

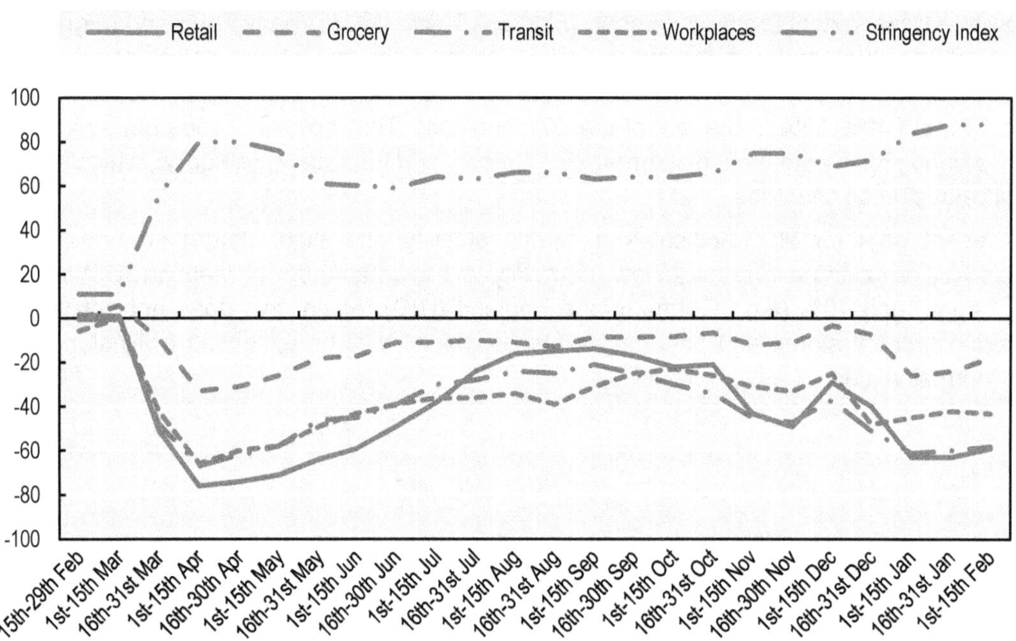

Note: See Figure 1.7 notes.
Source: Authors' elaboration based on (Google LLC, 2021[3]) and (Hale, T., S. Webster, A. Petherick, T. Phillips, and B. Kira, 2020a[5]).

StatLink https://doi.org/10.1787/888934248160

Figure 1.3. Mobility in G7 countries and strictness of lockdown policies, France

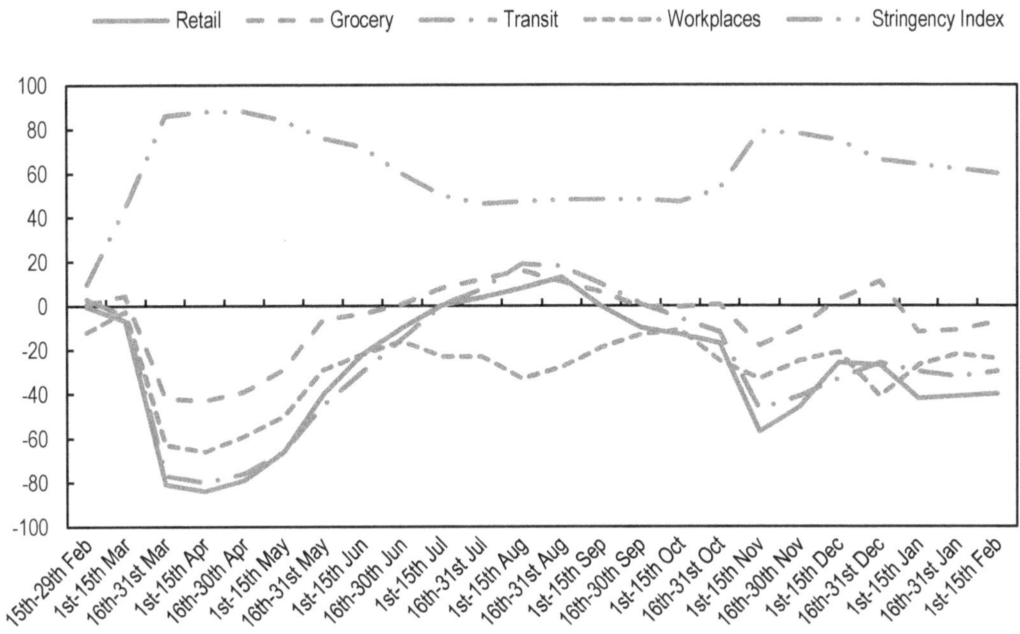

Note: See Figure 1.7 notes.
Source: Authors' elaboration based on (Google LLC, 2021[3]) and (Hale, T., S. Webster, A. Petherick, T. Phillips, and B. Kira, 2020a[5]).

StatLink https://doi.org/10.1787/888934248179

Figure 1.4. Mobility in G7 countries and strictness of lockdown policies, Germany

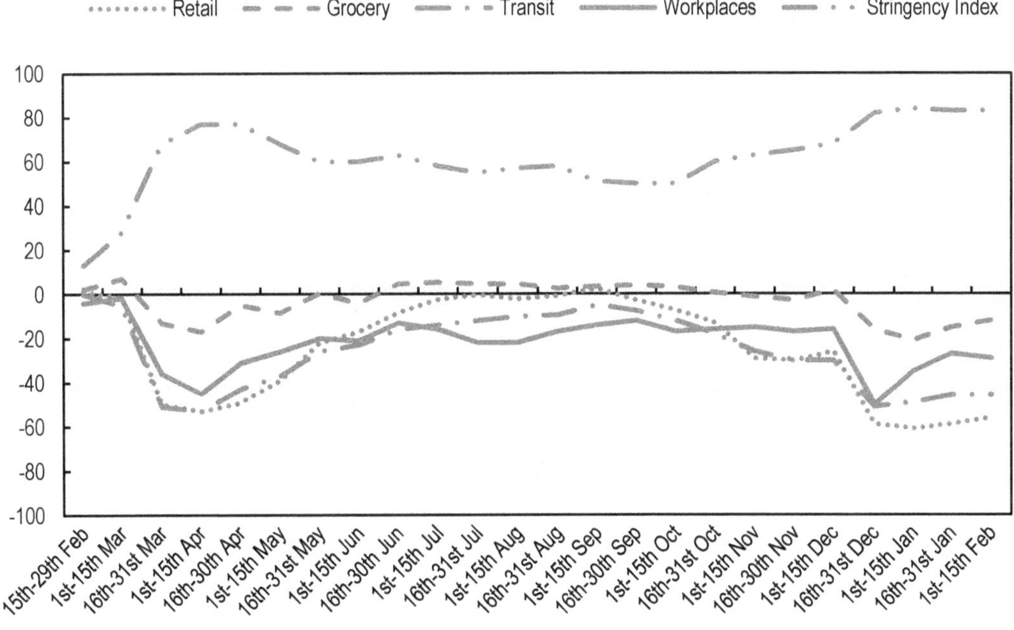

Note: See Figure 1.7 notes.
Source: Authors' elaboration based on (Google LLC, 2021[3]) and (Hale, T., S. Webster, A. Petherick, T. Phillips, and B. Kira, 2020a[5]).

StatLink https://doi.org/10.1787/888934248198

Figure 1.5. Mobility in G7 countries and strictness of lockdown policies, Italy

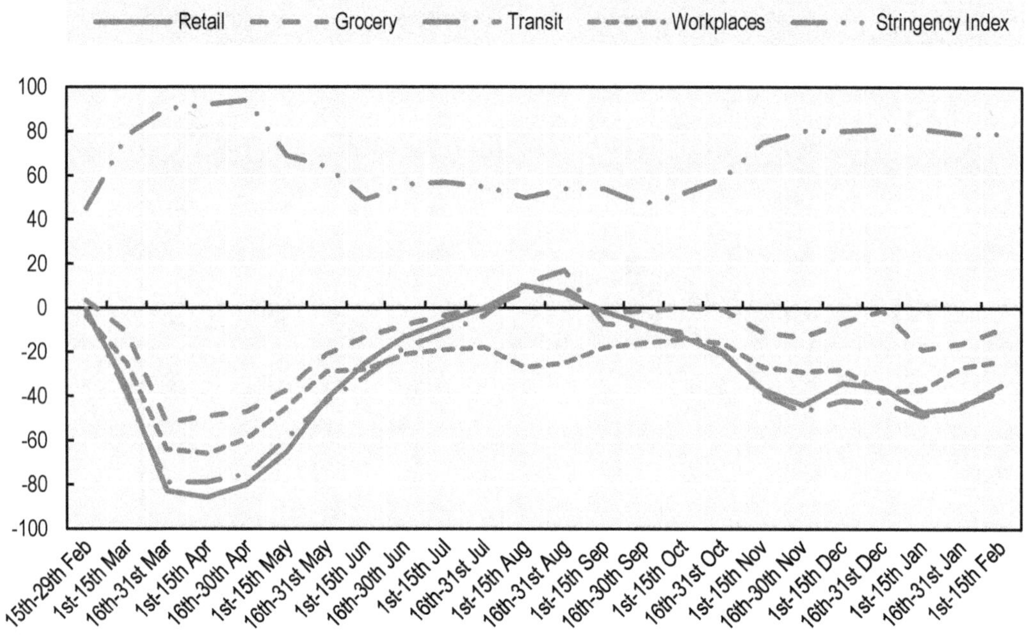

Note: See Figure 1.7 notes.
Source: Authors' elaboration based on (Google LLC, 2021[3]) and (Hale, T., S. Webster, A. Petherick, T. Phillips, and B. Kira, 2020a[5]).

StatLink https://doi.org/10.1787/888934248217

Figure 1.6. Mobility in G7 countries and strictness of lockdown policies, Japan

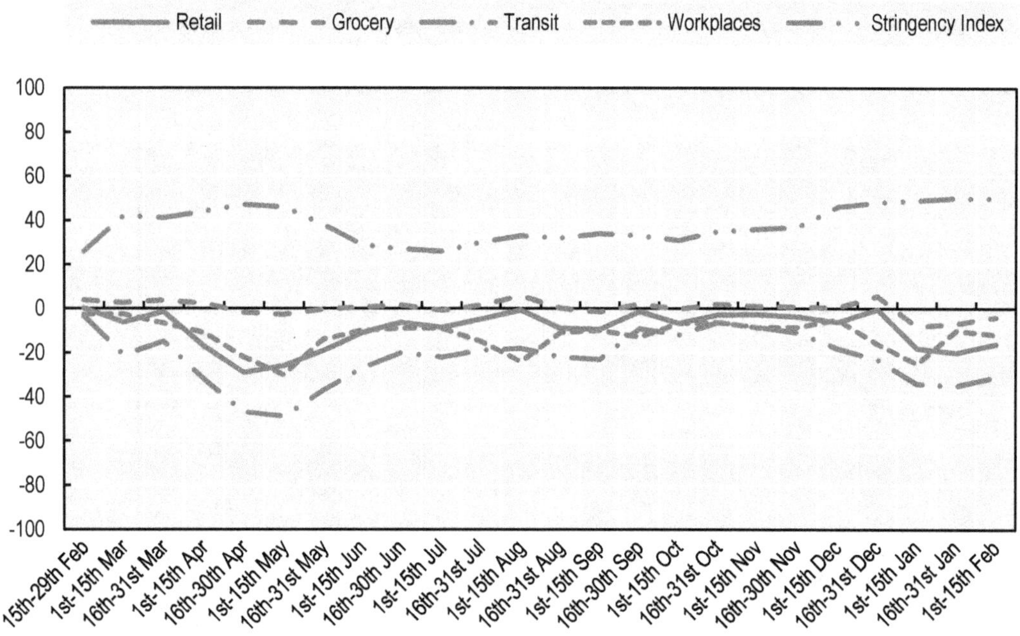

Note: See Figure 1.7 notes.
Source: Authors' elaboration based on (Google LLC, 2021[3]) and (Hale, T., S. Webster, A. Petherick, T. Phillips, and B. Kira, 2020a[5]).

StatLink https://doi.org/10.1787/888934248236

Figure 1.7. Mobility in G7 countries and strictness of lockdown policies, United States

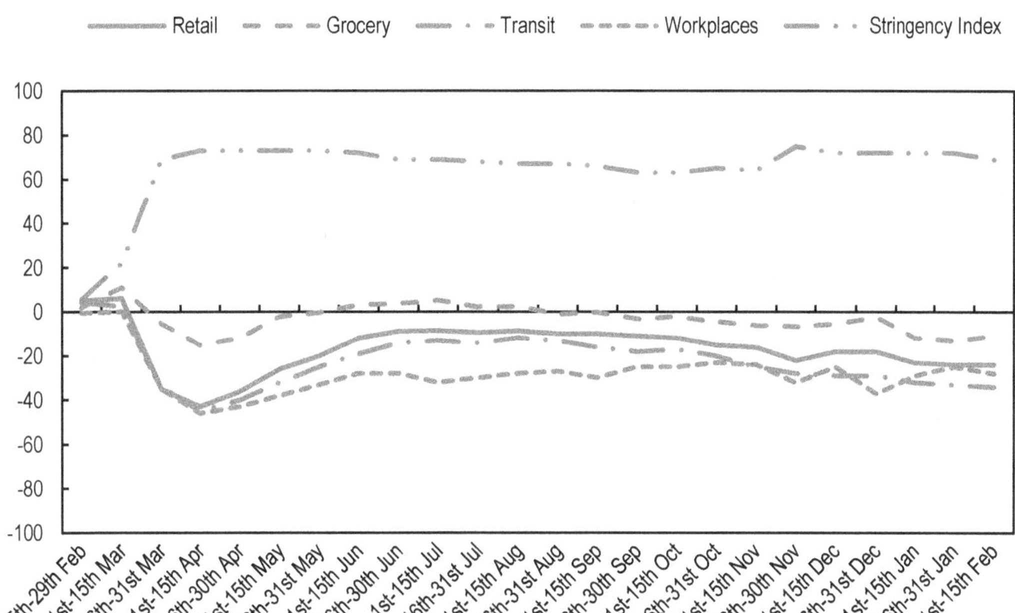

Note: Mobility values correspond to the average of the fortnight's means in the percentage change in mobility (from the median value for the corresponding day of the week from 3 January 2020 to 3 February period) to different places (Retail & Recreation, Grocery & Pharmacy, Transit Stations and Workplaces). The stringency index (dosh line) approximates the strictness of the "lockdown style" policies that (primarily) restrict people's behaviour.

Source: Authors' elaboration based on (Google LLC, 2021[3]) (regional mobility) and (Hale, T., S. Webster, A. Petherick, T. Phillips, and B. Kira, 2020a[5]).

StatLink https://doi.org/10.1787/888934248255

The evidence displays the expected negative association between mobility and lockdown policies, as the evolution of the "Stringency Index" largely mirrors that of mobility. After a clear jump around the month of March, the index started to decline in May, particularly in France, Italy and Japan, while it did so more softly in the remaining countries. It then rose again around November-December to reach March levels, or even higher, like in Japan and England (UK).

Workers' mobility seems to have been affected to a much greater extent than consumers' mobility throughout the period. When comparing different types of mobility, the only area that appeared to have "returned to normal" is the mobility around grocery stores and pharmacies. Across countries, Japan and the US appeared to be less affected than the other, and show more stability throughout the period. The European countries, on the other hand, appeared to have been more affected and showed deeper peaks in mobility (notably in the two drops observed in the period). Lastly, Canada lies somewhere in the middle in terms of both impact and peaks.

While the evidence suggests that lockdown policies were effective in restricting mobility, lockdown policies alone do not seem to explain mobility trends across countries. The correlation between increases in the stringency index and mobility drops is particularly high in the early period and/or when containment and closure policies were more severe. Nevertheless, the levels of the "Stringency Index" in Japan were substantially lower than in other countries: they were at nearly half of the levels reported for the European countries and substantially below those of the US and Canada. In fact, Japan declared a state of emergency, which implies softer lockdown policies than the ones generally imposed in Europe and the US.

This suggests that possibly other economic, technological and/or psychological factors contribute significantly to the observed differences in the impact of COVID-19 on people's mobility.

Mobility trends in large regions in G7 countries

Figures Figure 1.8 to Figure 1.14 illustrate the evolution of workplace mobility in TL2 regions of the G7 countries for the considered period. Annex 1.A includes the same figures for the four types of mobility.

While mobility patterns showed substantial variation across regions within each country, it is unclear what part of this variation can be attributed to COVID-19 related policies. The trends by regions show that, while the initial drop affected the regions of the same country in roughly the same way (i.e., in a magnitude similar to that observed for the whole country in the previous section), both the recovery and subsequent fall in mobility show substantial variation across regions of the same country. This is evident from the increasing dispersion in the regional trends after the initial shock. By mid-August 2020 many regions in different countries showed values around zero in consumers' mobility (see Annex 1.A), which means that they were (almost) back to normal levels of mobility. Some examples may help illustrate this point:

- In the US, both Rhode Island and Oklahoma were just below 5% in the percentage change of consumers' mobility with respect to the baseline period. In contrast, the District of Columbia showed mobility figures of around 50% below the values of the baseline period (in both consumers' and workers' mobility) (Figure 1.14).
- In Japan, values in "Grocery and Pharmacy" remained close to zero practically across the entire period, with average values in January 2020 at around 7% below the values of the baseline period. However, while regions like Tottori and Wakayama showed no difference in mobility levels with respect to the baseline period, the region of Okinawa was 13% below the values of the baseline period (Figure 1.20).

Figure 1.8. Commuting to workplaces in TL2 regions and Strictness of lockdown policies, Canada

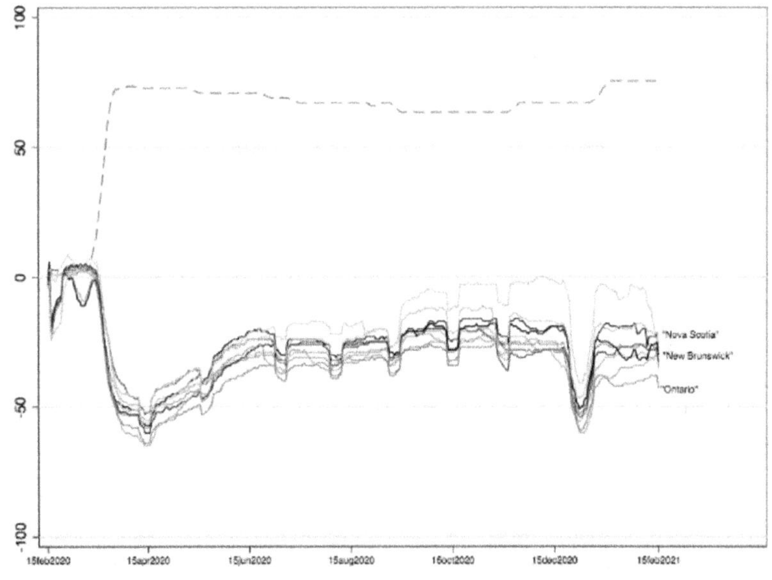

Note: See Figure 1.14 notes.
Source: Authors' elaboration based on (Google LLC, 2021[3]) and (Hale, T., S. Webster, A. Petherick, T. Phillips, and B. Kira, 2020a[5]).

Figure 1.9. Commuting to workplaces in TL2 regions and Strictness of lockdown policies, England (UK)

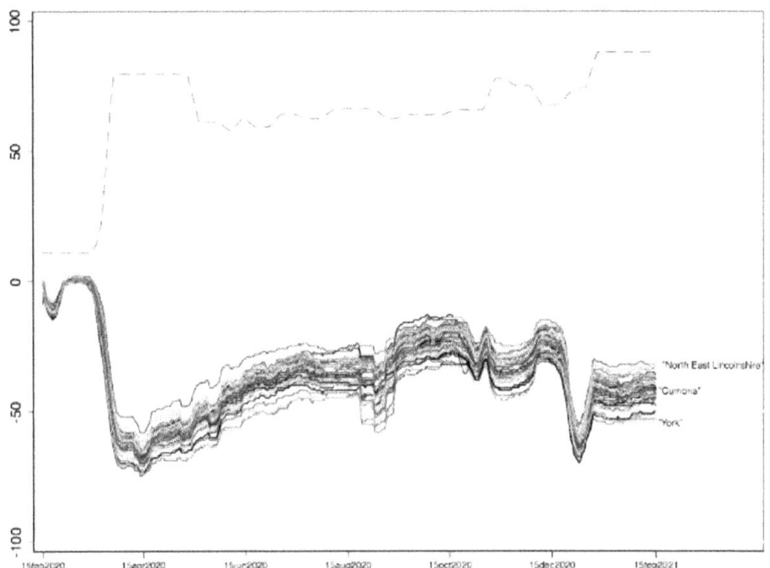

Note: See Figure 1.14 notes.
Source: Authors' elaboration based on (Google LLC, 2021[3]) and (Hale, T., S. Webster, A. Petherick, T. Phillips, and B. Kira, 2020a[5]).

Figure 1.10. Commuting to workplaces in TL2 regions and Strictness of lockdown policies, France

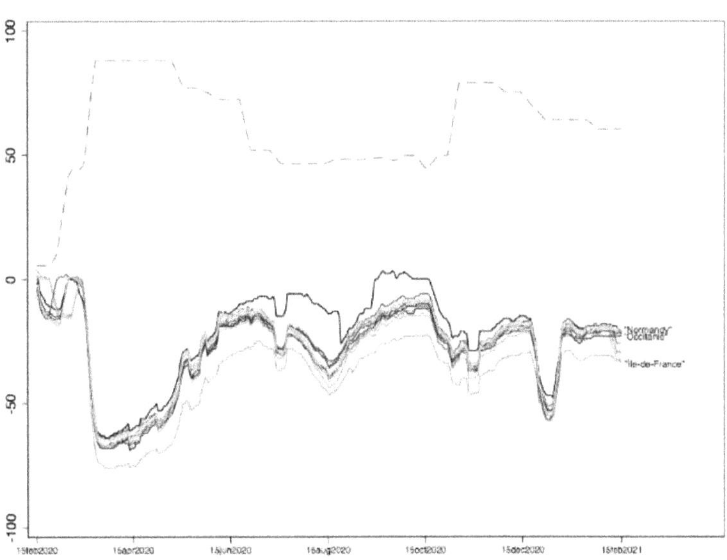

Note: See Figure 1.14 notes.
Source: Authors' elaboration based on (Google LLC, 2021[3]) and (Hale, T., S. Webster, A. Petherick, T. Phillips, and B. Kira, 2020a[5]).

Figure 1.11. Commuting to workplaces in TL2 regions and Strictness of lockdown policies, Germany

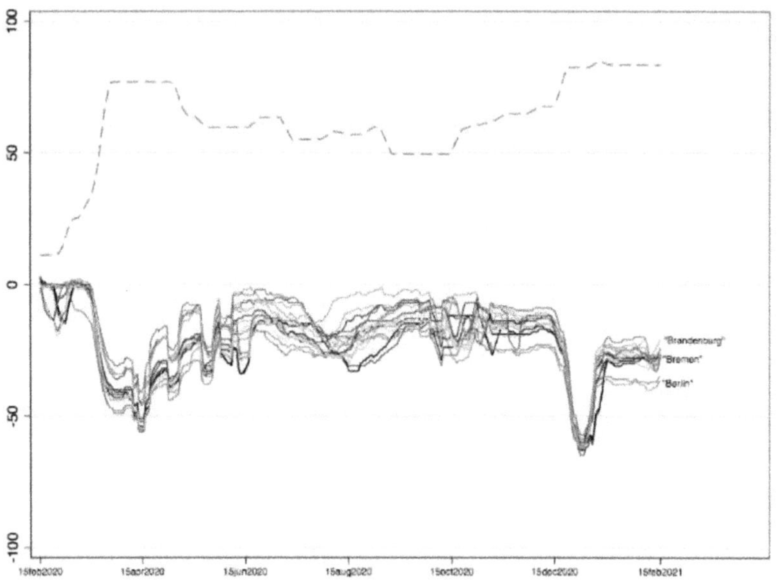

Note: See Figure 1.14 notes.
Source: Authors' elaboration based on (Google LLC, 2021[3]) and (Hale, T., S. Webster, A. Petherick, T. Phillips, and B. Kira, 2020a[5]).

Figure 1.12. Commuting to workplaces in TL2 regions and Strictness of lockdown policies, Italy

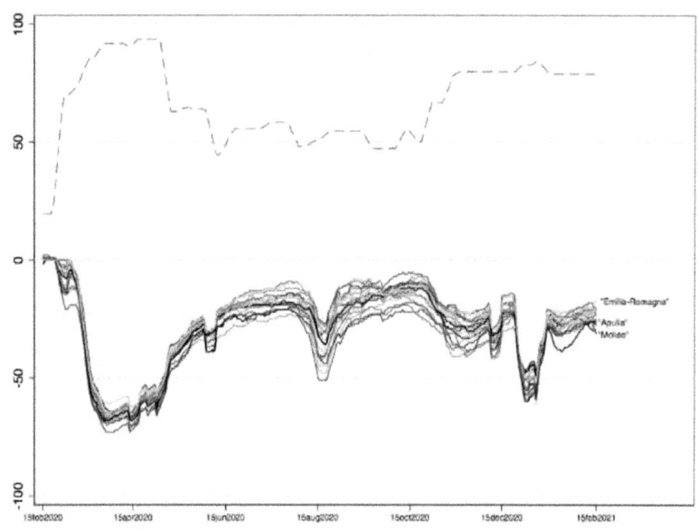

Note: See Figure 1.14 notes.
Source: Authors' elaboration based on (Google LLC, 2021[3]) and (Hale, T., S. Webster, A. Petherick, T. Phillips, and B. Kira, 2020a[5]).

Figure 1.13. Commuting to workplaces in TL2 regions and Strictness of lockdown policies, Japan

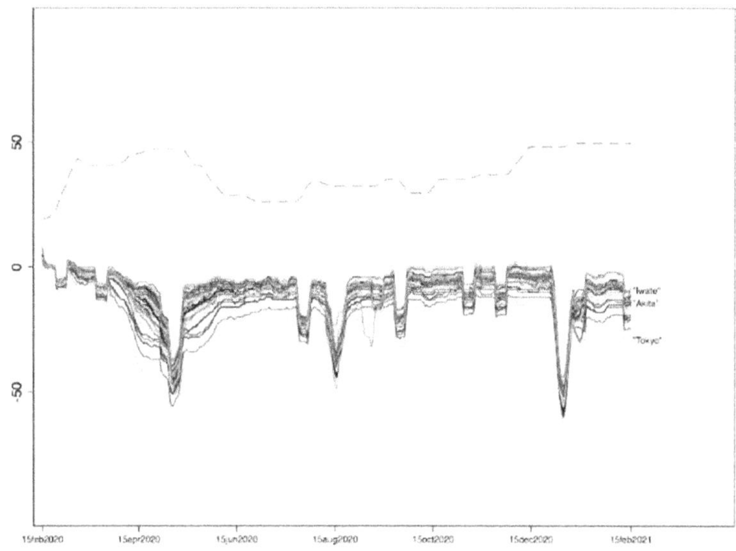

Note: See Figure 1.14 notes.
Source: Authors' elaboration based on (Google LLC, 2021[3]) and (Hale, T., S. Webster, A. Petherick, T. Phillips, and B. Kira, 2020a[5]).

Figure 1.14. Commuting to workplaces in TL2 regions and Strictness of lockdown policies, United States

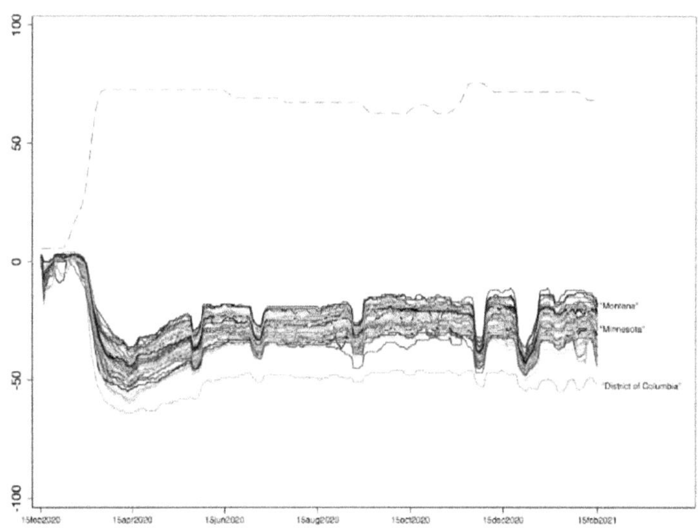

Note: Mobility values correspond to the percentage change mobility (from the median value for the corresponding day of the week from 3 January 2020 to 3 February) in mobility to Workplaces within the corresponding TL2 geographic area. The stringency index (dosh line) approximates the strictness of the "lockdown style" policies that (primarily) restrict people's behaviour.
Source: Authors' elaboration based on (Google LLC, 2021[3]) and (Hale, T., S. Webster, A. Petherick, T. Phillips, and B. Kira, 2020a[5]).

To focus on the relationship between mobility and regional characteristics, Table 1.1 summarises the three least and most affected regions in terms of average mobility[5], as well as in terms of GDP per capita, "teleworkability", and share of urban population. Teleworkability is measured as the estimated share of jobs that can potentially be performed at home[6] (Dingel, J. and Neiman, B., 2020[6]) (OECD, 2020[7]) and the share of urban population is measured as the percentage of people living in Functional Urban Areas (FUAs) in each TL2 region. For each country, three different moments are identified based on average mobility by fortnight:

- the minimum value between 15 February to 30 April 2020 (initial fall in mobility levels),
- the maximum value between in 1 May and 15 September 2020 (gradual recovery period) and,
- the minimum value between 16 September and 15 February 2021 (second drop in mobility levels).

The evidence suggests that factors related to the initial fall in relative mobility during the first wave (including not only containment policies but also possibly regional characteristics) continued to determine, to a large extent, mobility patterns in the rest of the period. Table 1.1 shows that, in many cases, the three most affected regions (i.e., the regions with the lowest relative mobility in the first shock compared to pre-COVID levels in January 2020, see first column), were on average more affected in the second wave (third column) and further away from "normal levels" during the recovery period (second column of the table). Similarly, the three least affected regions in terms of mobility in the initial shock were the least affected in the second wave (third column) and were the closest to "normal levels" during the recovery period. In other words, the ranking of mobility across regions within countries in the initial shock remained relatively stable throughout the year, including the second wave.

The composition of least and most affected regions in Table 1.1 suggests that the evolution of mobility and the return to normal may be related to certain characteristics of the regions. A comparison of the first three and last three columns of Table 1.1 for countries with available data[7] shows that the most affected regions in terms of mobility in the initial and second wave had, in many cases, the highest shares of tele-workability, urban share and, to a lesser extent, higher levels of GDP per capita. This association is observed for Quebec and Ontario in Canada (urban share); Hamburg, Bremen, Bavaria and Berlin in Germany (GDP per capita, remote working and urban share); Lombardy (GDP per capita and urban share) and Trentino-South Tyrol (GDP per capita) in Italy; Tokyo and Kanagawa in Japan (remote working); and District of Columbia (GDP per capita, remote working and urban share), New York (GDP per capita) and Massachusetts (GDP per capita, remote working) for the United States.

Table 1.1. Most and least affected three regions in average mobility during key dates and top and bottom regions in GDP per capita, remote working and rurality indices, G7 countries

Country	Initial wave	Progressive recovery	Second wave	GDP PC	Remote working	Urban share
Canada	**Least affected regions (lowest drop in mobility)**			**Top regions (highest rank)**		
	Nunavut	Prince Edward Island	Nunavut	Alberta	*Ontario*	*Ontario*
	Saskatchewan	Newfoundland and Labrador	Newfoundland and Labrador	Saskatchewan	British Columbia	*Quebec*
	Yukon	New Brunswick	Prince Edward Island	Newfoundland and Labrador	Quebec	Alberta
	Most affected regions (highest drop in mobility)			**Bottom regions (lowest rank)**		
	Quebec	Northwest Territories	Quebec	Prince Edward Island New	Prince Edward Island	Newfoundland and Labrador
	Ontario	Ontario	Ontario	Nova Scotia	Newfoundland and Labrador	Saskatchewan
	Nova Scotia	Yukon	Manitoba	New Brunswick	New Brunswick	Nova Scotia
France	**Least affected regions (lowest drop in mobility)**			**Top regions (highest rank)**		
	Corsica	Corsica	Corsica			
	Bourgogne-Franche-Comté	Nouvelle-Aquitaine	Nouvelle-Aquitaine			

	Provence-Alpes-Côte d'Azur	Brittany	Brittany			
	Most affected regions (highest drop in mobility)			**Bottom regions (lowest rank)**		
	Île-de-France	Île-de-France	Île-de-France			
	Grand Est	Hauts-de-France	Auvergne-Rhône-Alpes			
	Pays de la Loire	Grand Est	Hauts-de-France			
Germany	**Least affected regions (lowest drop in mobility)**			**Top regions (highest rank)**		
	Brandenburg	Mecklenburg-Vorpommern	Brandenburg	*Hamburg*	*Hamburg*	*Berlin*
	Thuringia	Schleswig-Holstein	Saxony-Anhalt	*Bremen*	*Berlin*	*Hamburg*
	Saxony-Anhalt	Brandenburg	Mecklenburg-Vorpommern	*Bavaria*	*Hesse*	*Bremen*
	Most affected regions (highest drop in mobility)			**Bottom regions (lowest rank)**		
	Saarland	Berlin	Berlin	Mecklenburg-Vorpomme	Mecklenburg-Vorpomme	Saxony-Anhalt
	Bavaria	Hamburg	Bavaria	Saxony-Anhalt	Saxony-Anhalt	Rhineland-Palatinate
	Hamburg	Bremen	Hesse	Brandenburg	Thuringia	Thuringia
Italy	**Least affected regions (lowest drop in mobility)**			**Top regions (highest rank)**		
	Sardinia	**Calabria**	Umbria	*Lombardy*	Lazio	Lazio
	Umbria	Aosta	Abruzzo	*Trentino-South Tyrol*	*Lombardy*	Campania
	Molise	Molise	Calabria	Aosta Valley	Liguria	*Lombardy*
	Most affected regions (highest drop in mobility)			**Bottom regions (lowest rank)**		
	Lombardy	Lombardy	Aosta	**Calabria**	Basilicata	Marche
	Trentino-South Tyrol	Calabria	Veneto	Sicily	Calabria	Abruzzo
	Calabria	Piedmont	Lombardy	Campania	Abruzzo	Calabria
Japan	**Least affected regions (lowest drop in mobility)**			**Top regions (highest rank)**		
	Akita	Fukui	Tokushima		*Tokyo*	
	Aomori	Yamagata	Iwate		*Kanagawa*	
	Iwate	Akita	Kagawa		Shimane	
	Most affected regions (highest drop in mobility)			**Bottom regions (lowest rank)**		
	Tokyo	Tokyo	Tokyo		Kagawa	
	Okinawa	Okinawa	Osaka		Kagoshima	
	Kanagawa	Osaka	Ishikawa		Kochi	
United Kingdom (UK)	**Least affected regions (lowest drop in mobility)**			**Top regions (highest rank)**		
	North Lincolnshire	Cornwall	North Lincolnshire			
	East Riding of Yorkshire	Isle of Wight	North East Lincolnshire			
	Redcar and Cleveland	Blackpool	Torbay			
	Most affected regions (highest drop in mobility)			**Bottom regions (lowest rank)**		
	Bath and North East Somerset	Reading	Bath and North East Somerset			
	Reading	Bristol City	Brighton and Hove			
	York	Nottingham	Reading			
United States (US)	**Least affected regions (lowest drop in mobility)**			**Top regions (highest rank)**		
	Arkansas	South Dakota	South Dakota	*District of*	*District of*	*District of*

			Columbia	*Columbia*	*Columbia*
Wyoming	Wyoming	Idaho	*New York*	*Massachusetts*	New Jersey
Oklahoma	Montana	Montana	*Massachusetts*	New Jersey	California
Most affected regions (highest drop in mobility)			**Bottom regions (lowest rank)**		
District of Columbia	District of Columbia	District of Columbia	Mississippi	Mississippi	New Hampshire
New York	Hawaii	Massachusetts	West Virginia	West Virginia	West Virginia
Hawaii	Florida	New York	Arkansas	Wyoming	Mississippi

Note: Most/least regions in mean mobility changes calculated as the average of the fortnight's means in "Retail and Recreation", "Grocery and Pharmacy", "Transit Stations" and "Workplaces". Selected fortnights correspond to those with the lower mean-country value in the period 15 February to 30 April, the higher mean-country value in the period from 1 May to 15 September and the lower mean-country value from 16 September to 15 February. For Canada: 1-15 April 2020, 16-30 June 2020 and 1-15 January 2021; for France: 1-15- April 2020, 1-15 August 2020 and 1-15 November 2020; for Germany: 1-15- April 2020, 1-15 September 2020 and 16-31 December 2020; for Italy: 1-15- April 2020, 1-15 August and 1-15 January 2020; for Japan 1-15 May 2020, 16-30 September 2020 and 1-15 January 2020; for England (UK): 1-15- April 2020, 16-30 September 2020 and 1-15 January 2020; for US: 1-15- April 2020, 1-15 August 2020 and 1-15 February 2020.
Source: Authors' elaboration based on (Google LLC, 2021[3]) (regional mobility). Own computations using data from (OECD, 2021[8]) (GDP per capita and degree of rurality), (Dingel, J. and Neiman, B., 2020[6]), (OECD, 2020[7]) and Ministry of Land, Infrastructure, Transport and Tourism (share of jobs that can potentially be performed at home).

Rural-urban differences using Mapbox activity data

This section uses Mapbox mobility data to analyse trends below the TL2-level for two countries with available data: US and Germany. The first part briefly discusses data processing. The next part shows national trends compared to the trend in cases in both countries, and the last part discusses the rural-urban comparison for both countries.

Data sources and processing

The analysis in this section is based on the Activity Index derived from Mapbox Movement data for the period 1 January 2020 to 31 December 2020 for two countries with available data: the US and Germany. Mapbox movement data is built from mobile device users and captures significant driving and non-driving mobile device activity. Unlike the Google data, the Mapbox movement data does not distinguish between types of mobility (e.g. consumer vs workplaces). On the other hand, it allows for finer geographical detail suitable for territorial comparisons.

The analysis obtains an indicator of overall activity in a country by summing activity index values observed at the local level (county for US and *Landkreis* (TL3) for Germany). To compare trends across regions with different degrees of rurality, the analysis aggregates the movement data for Germany into region types according to the OECD regional typology based on access to cities (Fadic et al., 2019[9]) (see Box 1.1). For the US, as data are available at the county level, the rural-urban analysis uses the 2013 Rural-Urban Continuum Codes from the Economic Research Service of the United States Department of Agriculture.[8] For the analysis, the eight original codes have been collapsed into four categories: metro; non-metro adjacent to metro with urban population; non-metro non-adjacent to metro with urban population; and non-metro completely rural.

Box 1.1. Classifying TL3 regions by their level of access to cities

The EU-OECD regional classification based on access takes into consideration the presence of and access to a Functional Urban Area (FUA). Access is defined in terms of the time needed to reach the closest urban area, which takes into account not only geographical features but also the status of physical road infrastructure.

The typology classifies TL3 regions into metropolitan and non-metropolitan according to the following criteria:

Metropolitan TL3 region (MR), if more than 50% of its population live in a FUA of at least 250 000 inhabitants.

Non-metropolitan TL3 region (NMR), if less than 50% of its population live in a FUA. NMRs are further classified according to their level of access to FUAs of different sizes into:

- ***Near a city > 250 000***, if more than 50% of its population lives within a 45-minute drive from a metropolitan area (a FUA with more than 250 000 people); or if the TL3 region contains more than 80% of the area of a FUA of at least 250 000 inhabitants.
- ***With/near a city <250 000***, if the TL3 region does not have access to a metro and 50% of its population has access to a small or medium city (a FUA of more than 50 000 and less than 250 000 inhabitants) within a 60-minute drive; or if the TL3 region contains more than 80% of the area of a small or medium city.
- ***Remote region***, if the TL3 region is not classified as NMR-M or NMR-S, i.e. if 50% of its population does not have access to any FUA within a 60-minute drive.

Source: (Fadic et al., 2019[9]). Classifying small (TL3) regions based on metropolitan population, low density and remoteness. OECD Regional Development Working Papers, 2019/06, OECD, Paris.

Importantly, the activity index is not scaled to population, so the size of the country or local unit (e.g. as measured by its population) affects the index. In other words, an increase in activity represents more of a change in a high-density place than in a low-density place. For this reason, the analysis focuses on trends over time and does not compare change rates across places or countries.

Box 1.2. Constructing the Mapbox activity index

The Movement Activity Index is constructed from anonymous location events transmitted from mobile devices with at least one mobile app installed that uses the Mapbox Mobile SDK. These location traces are aggregated into spatial grids of approximately 100m² in size.

A normalisation period is set to January 2020 to calculate an average daily activity level over that period for each app. The activity index varies between 0 and 1. Activity = 1 represents the maximum activity observed in a country during the baseline period January 2020. This maximum activity is likely to occur in a densely populated area (for instance the busiest district of New York City). The majority of Activity Index values will fall into the ranges 0-0.3 because most places show activity levels that are well below those of the main activity centre – even during pre-COVID levels.

Source: (Mapbox, 2021[4]).

National trends in activity

While the scale of activity differs across countries (highest for US, lowest for Germany), focusing on trends over 2020 shows that, compared to Germany, the US experienced a deeper, more sudden drop in activity at the start of the pandemic crisis in March (Figure 1.15). The largest fall in the activity index in the US occurred in the last week of March, coinciding with the first peak in the number of cases and stay-at-home orders issued on 20 March in New York City. At the same time, the activity index started steadily declining in Germany in early March, reflecting start of the first wave and restrictions affecting mobility that were put in place in mid-March.

While the recovery after the first wave was much slower in Germany than in the US, both countries had regained some of their activity levels by early July – although levels remained markedly below those observed before the pandemic (Figure 1.15 and Figure 1.16). Both countries experienced reductions in activity levels again in late October that lasted through the end of the year, as the second wave emerged in both countries. The relative drop in activity compared to the increase in cases was evidently stronger in Germany than in the US.

These results are in line with those shown by the Google trends data; however the Mapbox data shows a steeper decline in activity in the US in the closing months of 2020.

Figure 1.15. Country-level trends in activity, United States

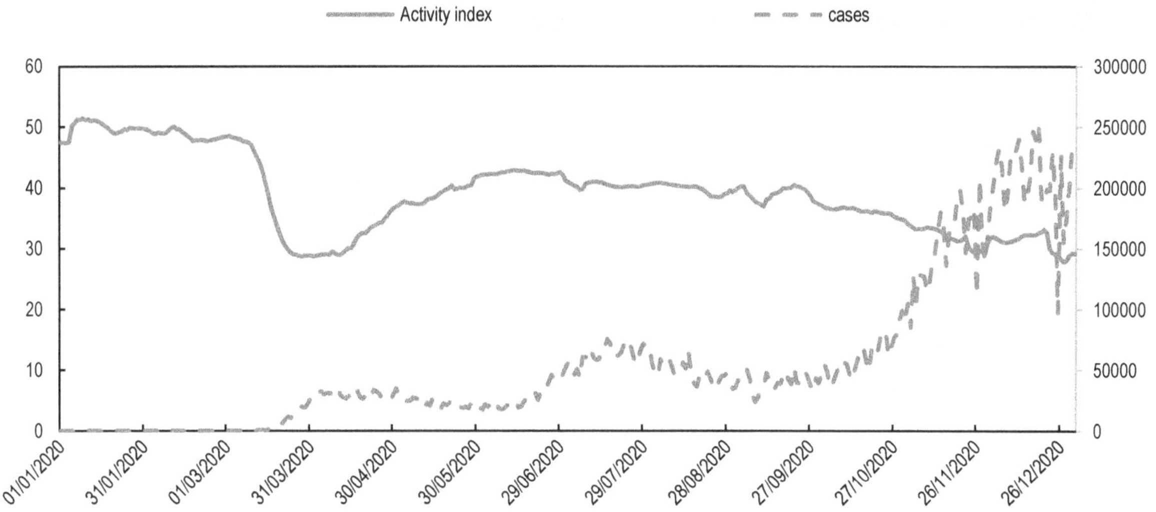

Note: 7-day moving average.
Source: Author's elaboration using (Mapbox, 2021[4]).

StatLink https://doi.org/10.1787/888934248274

Figure 1.16. Country-level trends in activity, Germany

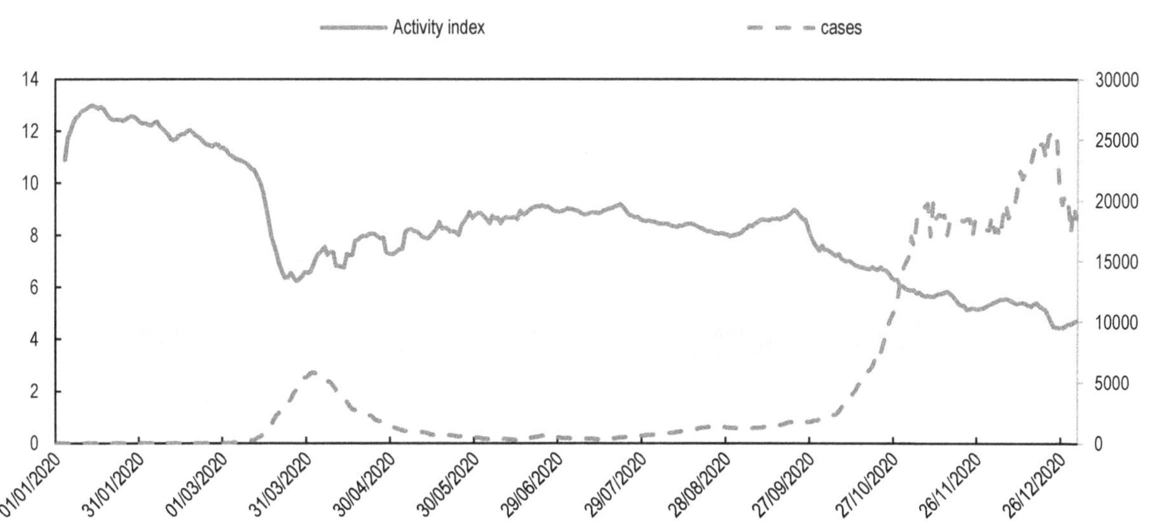

Note: 7-day moving average.
Source: Author's elaboration using (Mapbox, 2021[4]).

StatLink https://doi.org/10.1787/888934248293

Metropolitan/non-metropolitan differences in Germany and the US

Were falls in activity disproportionally higher in metropolitan regions (especially those with a very large city)? And did non-metropolitan regions around metropolitan regions show more resilience or even increases in activity that could be potentially linked to people inflows? To get a sense of the impact in the months following the shock of the first wave in metropolitan versus non-metropolitan regions, Figure 1.17 and Figure 1.20 compare the activity index across California, Texas and Vermont in the US, and Bavaria, North Rhine-Westphalia and Hesse in Germany between a day before the first wave shock (Thursday 30 January 2020) and a day after the impact of the first wave had subsided (Thursday 28 May 2020).

In the US, the comparison suggests that the regions with the largest drops in mobility were large metropolitan regions, while many smaller metropolitan regions maintained their activity levels at similar levels in May 2020 compared to January 2020. Changes in activity levels in non-metropolitan regions are not evident in these maps as they have much lower levels compared to metropolitan regions. The most visible activity drops in May compared to pre-COVID-19 concentrated in Los Angeles and the Silicon Valley area including San Francisco and Sacramento, while smaller metropolitan regions including San Diego do not show changes that are as large (Figure 1.17). In Texas, while a drop in activity is only visible in Houston and Dallas, the strip of metropolitan areas between Dallas and San Antonio, including Austin, showed similar levels of mobility in May 2020 compared to January 2020 (Figure 1.18). Finally, Vermont shows little variation in activity levels between the two periods, although it is worth noting that initial activity index levels were much smaller in this smaller, less urban state (Figure 1.19).

Figure 1.17. Comparison of activity index between January and May 2020, California (US)

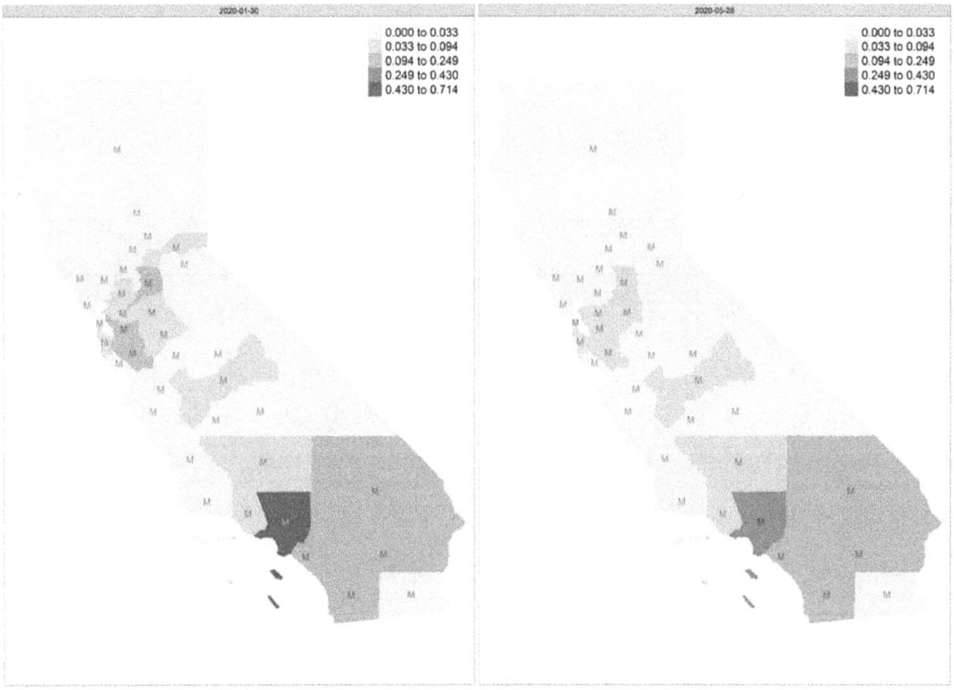

Note: M indicates Metropolitan Region. Regions with no label are non-metropolitan regions.
Source: Author's elaboration using (Mapbox, 2021[4]).

Figure 1.18. Comparison of activity index between January and May 2020, Texas (US)

Note: M indicates Metropolitan Region. Regions with no label are non-metropolitan regions.
Source: Author's elaboration using (Mapbox, 2021[4]).

Figure 1.19. Comparison of activity index between January and May 2020, Vermont (US)

Note: M indicates Metropolitan Region. Regions with no label are non-metropolitan regions.
Source: Author's elaboration using (Mapbox, 2021[4]).

In the selected regions of Germany, activity levels in non-metropolitan regions were not always below those of metropolitan regions to start with, so the changes between January 2020 and May 2020 concern both types of regions. In Bavaria, the fall of activity in the large metropolitan region of Munich coincided with falls in activity in most of the larger economic cluster of manufacturing and ICT industries surrounding the region that covers Nuremberg in the North, Augsburg in the West and the South border, much like the larger economic area around Nuremberg (Figure 1.20). A similar trend is observed in the Ruhr valley in North Rhine-Westphalia centred on Düsseldorf, the most important industrial cluster of Germany that also includes non-metropolitan regions. In this area, the drop in activity in the large metropolitan area of Düsseldorf coincided with similar drops in activity in surrounded areas, compatible with the high level of inter-connection in these areas (Figure 1.21). Finally, in Hesse—besides the drop in activity in Frankfurt and the regions surrounding it—the data does not show higher activity levels in non-metropolitan regions but rather a drop in activity in those areas that had relatively high levels to start with (Figure 1.22).

The trends for Germany are consistent with a drop in general activity in these regions that was largest in large metropolitan regions. Unlike the US, in Germany the drop may have affected both metropolitan and non-metropolitan regions. The data however does not lend support to increases in activity outside metropolitan regions that could potentially compensate for the decrease in activity in cities, at least in the months following the first wave shock.

Figure 1.20. Comparison of activity index between January and May 2020, Bavaria (Germany)

Note: M indicates Metropolitan Region. Regions with no label are non-metropolitan regions.
Source: Author's elaboration using (Mapbox, 2021[4]).

Figure 1.21. Comparison of activity index between January and May 2020, North Rhine-Westphalia (Germany)

Note: M indicates Metropolitan Region. Regions with no label are non-metropolitan regions.
Source: Author's elaboration using (Mapbox, 2021[4]).

Figure 1.22. Comparison of activity index between January and May 2020, Hesse (Germany)

Note: M indicates Metropolitan Region. Regions with no label are non-metropolitan regions.
Source: Author's elaboration using (Mapbox, 2021[4]).

Rural-urban differences in activity in Germany and the US

To identify possible outliers to national trends and their location Figure 1.23 compares the total and maximum activity by type of region in Germany. The analysis of maximum activity focuses only on non-metropolitan regions because metropolitan regions have much higher levels of activity throughout the year.

In Germany, activity levels of regions near or with small/medium cities are closer to levels in remote regions than to levels of regions near a large city (Figure 1.23). Even so, the maximum activity levels are recorded in remote regions in certain weeks during the summer and early fall, and in regions near a large city in January-June and November-December. Then, activity starts decelerating in October, although the fall in Germany is stronger and more even across the different types of regions. This trend coincides with nationally enforced strict regulations regarding mobility as well as school and business closures.

Figure 1.23. Total activity index by type of TL3 region and maximum activity in non-metropolitan regions, Germany

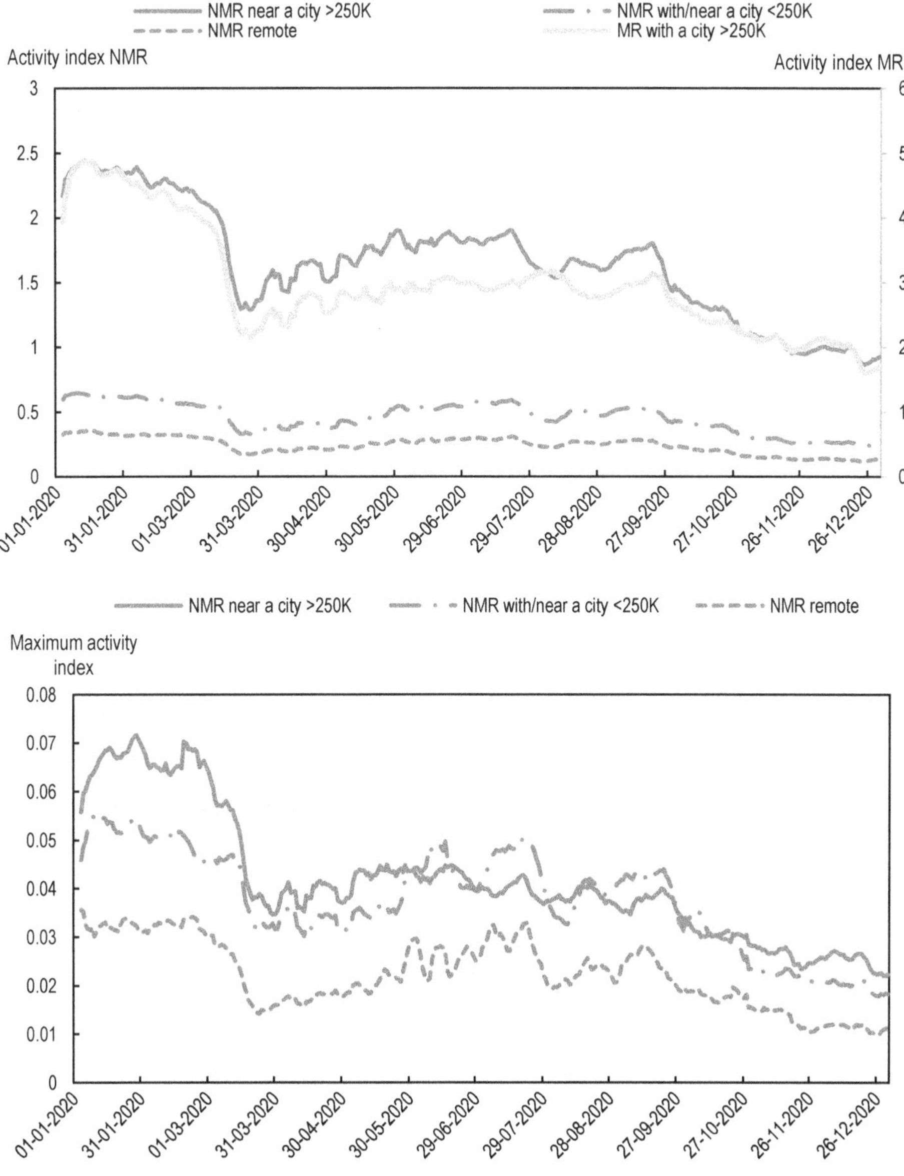

Note: 7-day moving average
Source: Author's elaboration using (Mapbox, 2021[4]).

StatLink https://doi.org/10.1787/888934248312

The evidence for the US, based on country-level data, indicates that the hierarchy in mobility (from highest mobility levels in more urban places and lowest in more rural places) is maintained throughout 2020. While the data offers little support to the idea of permanent changes in activity in counties in those states during 2020, it shows that non-metro counties with an urban population adjacent to metro areas experienced a smaller fall in mobility levels and a better recovery after the first wave than metro counties **(**Figure 1.24). The resilience of non-metro counties adjacent to cities is evident in the trends for counties with the highest mobility levels, as both adjacent and non-adjacent metro counties with an urban population had similar maximum mobility levels until May; however, after May, adjacent counties stayed above the rest of non-metro counties throughout 2020.

Figure 1.24. Total activity index by type of county and maximum activity in non-metropolitan counties, US

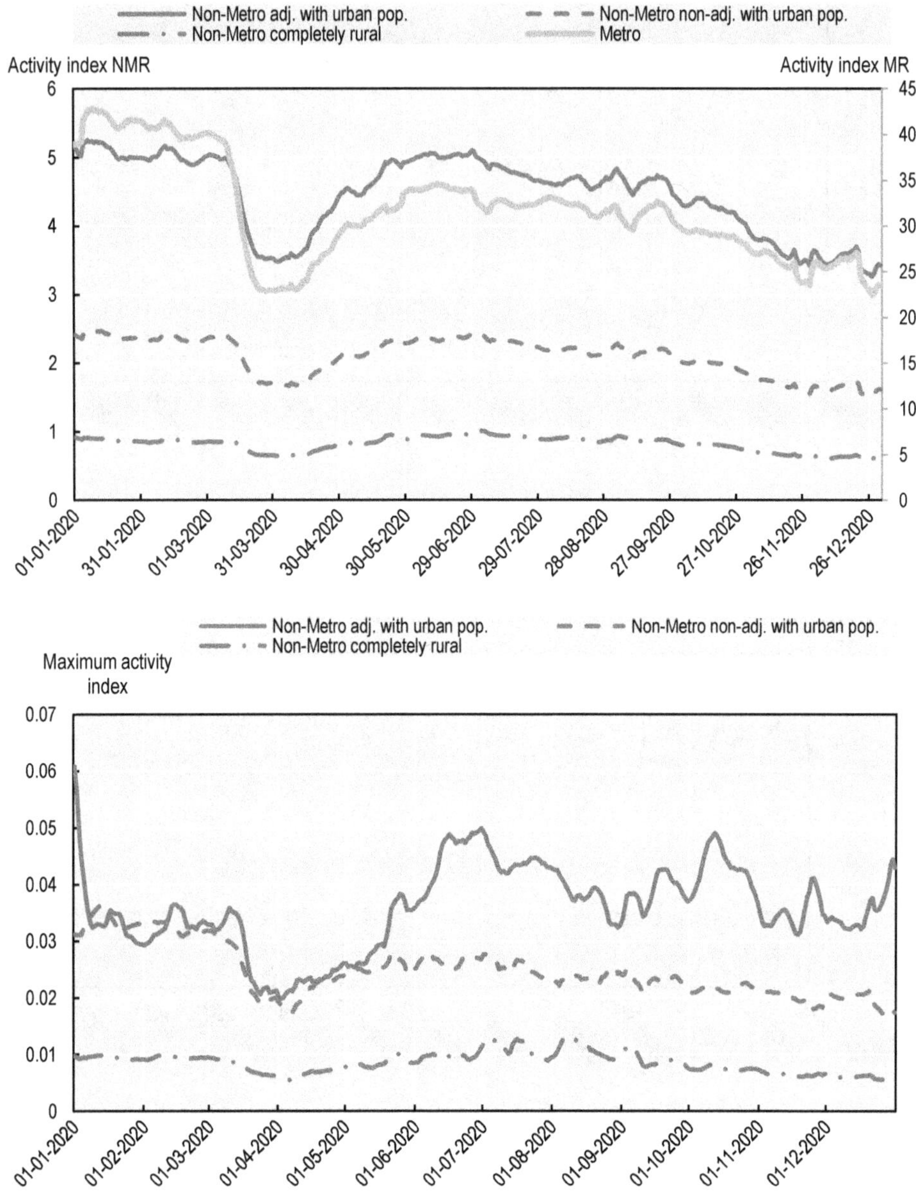

Note: 7-day moving average
Source: Author's elaboration using (Mapbox, 2021[4]).

StatLink https://doi.org/10.1787/888934248331

Conclusions

Returning to the initial questions (i.e., How much has COVID-19 affected the daily mobility of people, especially in relation to their home-work movements? Has this impact been different for urban or rural areas?) the evidence in this chapter suggests that throughout 2020 and early 2021 the COVID-19 pandemic has had a sustained impact on mobility, with some relief during the summer months. The impact has been stronger on regions with large cities that had the highest levels of mobility to start with, both during the first and second waves. As the Google data suggests, this could be mostly linked to reduced work-related mobility.

The evidence in this chapter does not support a clear increase in activity in rural areas following the decrease in activity in cities, but instead suggests that mobility levels are still far from normal everywhere. At the same time, both mobility trends and regional variation within countries do not seem to be explained by containment policies alone. The evidence in this chapter showed that the ranking of mobility across regions within countries in the initial shock stayed relatively stable throughout the year, including the second shock. This implies that the weight of initial characteristics may be difficult to overcome through differentiated policies at least while the pandemic continues to unfold.

References

Chetty, R. et al. (2020), *The Economic Impacts of COVID-19: Evidence from a New Public Database Built Using*, https://opportunityinsights.org/wp-content/uploads/2020/05/tracker_paper.pdf (accessed on march 2021). [1]

Dingel, J. and Neiman, B. (2020), *How many jobs can be done at home?*, COVID Economics: Vetted and Real-Time Papers, 1, https://cepr.org/sites/default/files/news/CovidEcon1%20final.pdf. [6]

Fadic, M. et al. (2019), "Classifying small (TL3) regions based on metropolitan population, low density and remoteness", *OECD Regional Development Working Papers*, No. 2019/06, OECD Publishing, Paris, https://dx.doi.org/10.1787/b902cc00-en. [9]

Google (2021), *COVID-19 Community Mobility Reports (regional mobility values)*, https://www.google.com/covid19/mobility/ (accessed on February 2021). [10]

Google LLC (2021), *Google COVID-19 Community Mobility Reports*, https://www.google.com/covid19/mobility/ (accessed on March 2021). [3]

Hale, T., S. Webster, A. Petherick, T. Phillips, and B. Kira (2020a), *Oxford COVID-19 Government Response Tracker*, Blavatnik School of Government. [5]

Mapbox (2021), *Mapbox Movement data*, https://www.mapbox.com/movement-data (accessed on June 2020). [4]

OECD (2021), *OECD regional statistics*, https://www.oecd.org/regional/regional-statistics/ (accessed on February 2021). [8]

OECD (2020), *Capacity for remote working can affect lockdown costs differently across places*, OECD Policy Responses to Coronavirus, https://www.oecd.org/coronavirus/policy-responses/capacity-for-remote-working-can-affect-lockdown-costs-differently-across-places-0e85740e/. [7]

Pareliussen, J. and D. Glocker (2021), *Lockdown policies and people in the age of COVID-19: Lessons from the OECD Policy Tracker*, https://oecdecoscope.blog/2020/07/07/lockdown-policies-and-people-in-the-age-of-covid-19-lessons-from-the-oecd-policy-tracker/ (accessed on March 2021). [2]

Notes

[1] These data are available at:
https://www.gstatic.com/covid19/mobility/Global_Mobility_Report.csv?cachebust=7d0cb7d254d29111
and are calculated using data from Google users that have opted-in to Location History for their Google Account. This means that while they may reflect major trends in people's mobility they may not be representative of the behaviour of the whole population in the geographical area considered.

[2] "Parks" and "Residential" are other places considered in the Global Mobility Report of Google but not analysed here.

[3] The analysis is limited to TL2 regions because, at the time of access, information on TL3 regions was only available for Canada, France, Italy and Japan. In fact, data for Japan was only available for TL3 units ("prefectures") and data for England was available for "local authorities" and "districts". In any case, using lower levels of aggregation may obscure the graphical representation (in England, for example, using district data would mean plotting around 1 700 lines) while it is unlikely to result in informative differences in trends.

[4] These data are available at the national level (and the US states) and consist of a set of indicators of government policies on containment and closure (C1 to C8 indicators), economy (E1 to E4 indicators) and health (H1 to H5 indicators). The reported index is the average of C1 to C8 indicators. All data is available at: https://raw.githubusercontent.com/OxCGRT/covid-policy-tracker/master/data/OxCGRT_latest.csv

[5] Average mobility is the mean of the four mobility types for each country and fortnight. Using each area of mobility instead of the mean of the four dimension leads to essentially the same conclusions.

[6] Data for Japan provided by the Ministry of Land, Infrastructure, Transport and Tourism.

[7] For France, Japan and England it was not possible to match the territorial units in the Google data with those in (OECD, 2021[8]).

[8] https://www.ers.usda.gov/data-products/rural-urban-continuum-codes/

Annex 1.A. Mobility in TL2 regions and Strictness of lockdown policies

Annex Figure 1.A.1. Mobility in TL2 regions and Strictness of lockdown policies, Canada

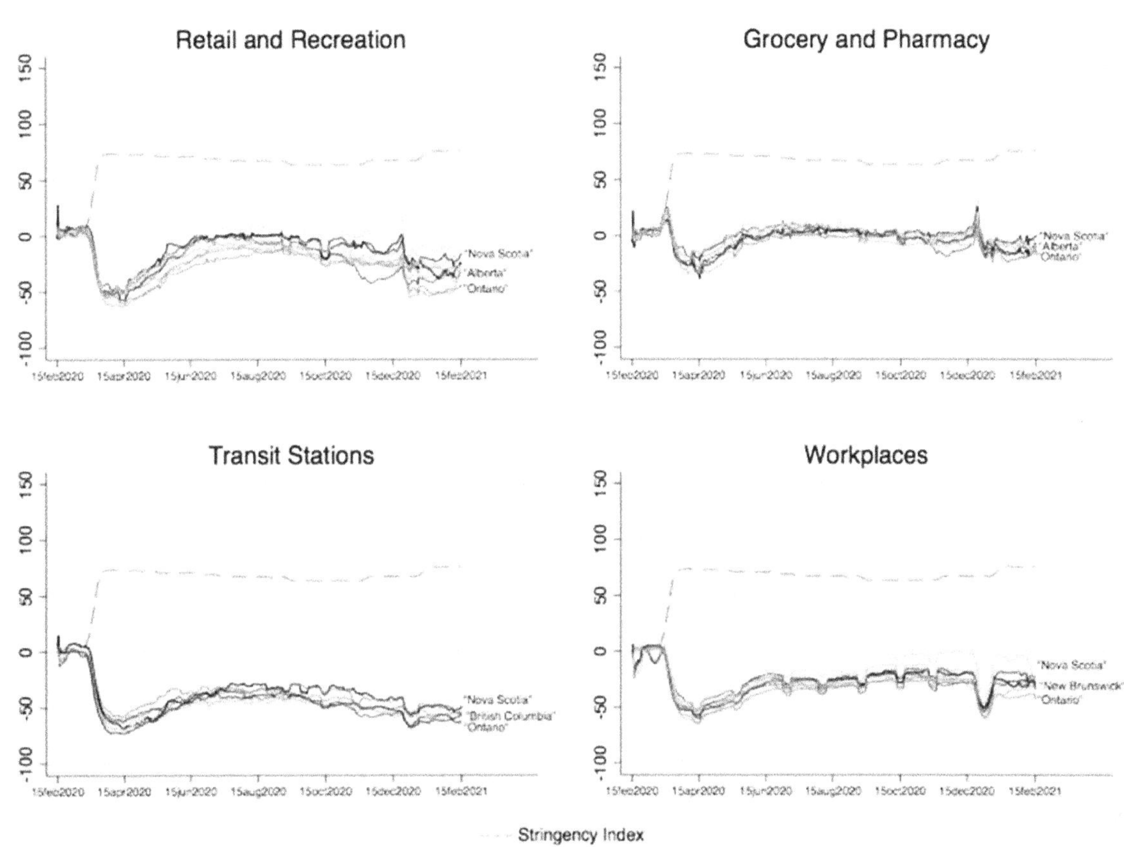

Note: See notes Annex Figure 1.A.7.
Source: Authors' elaboration based on (Google LLC, 2021[3]) and (Hale, T., S. Webster, A. Petherick, T. Phillips, and B. Kira, 2020a[5]).

Annex Figure 1.A.2. Mobility in TL2 regions and Strictness of lockdown policies, England (UK)

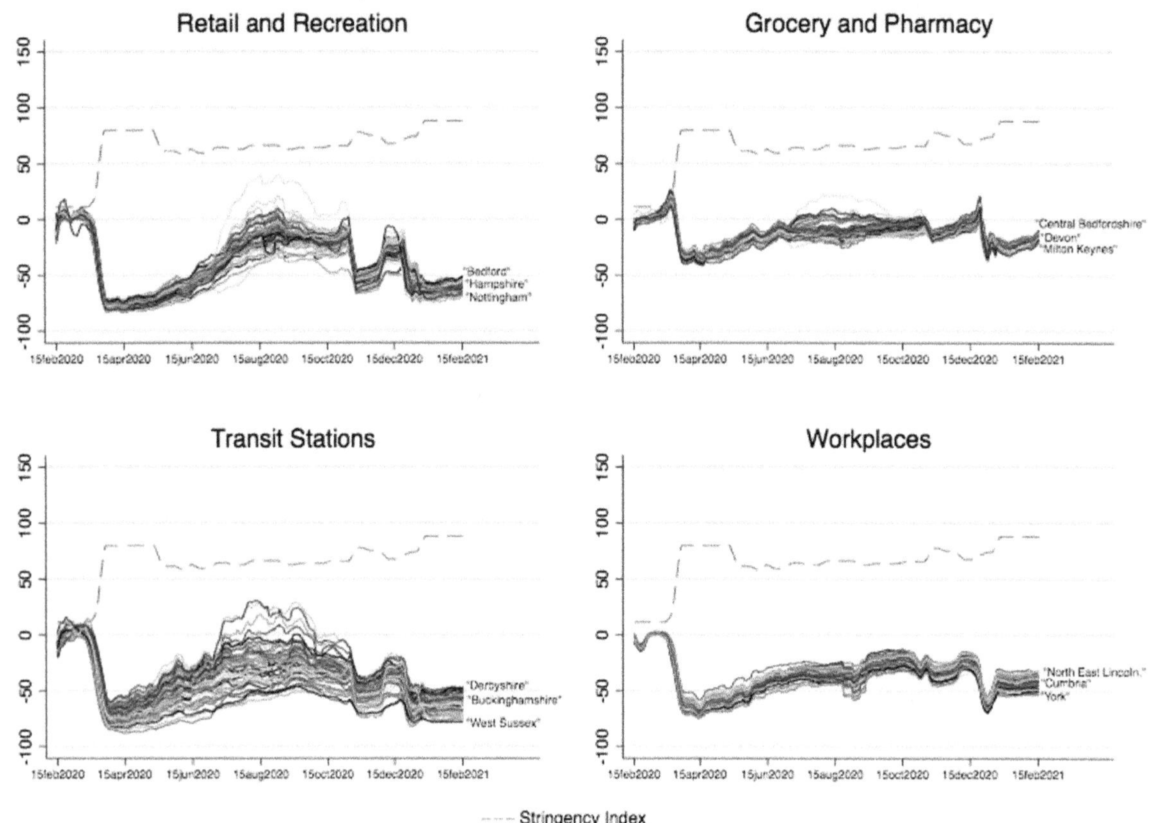

Note: See notes Annex Figure 1.A.7.
Source: Authors' elaboration based on (Google LLC, 2021[3]) and (Hale, T., S. Webster, A. Petherick, T. Phillips, and B. Kira, 2020a[5]).

Annex Figure 1.A.3. Mobility in TL2 regions and Strictness of lockdown policies, France

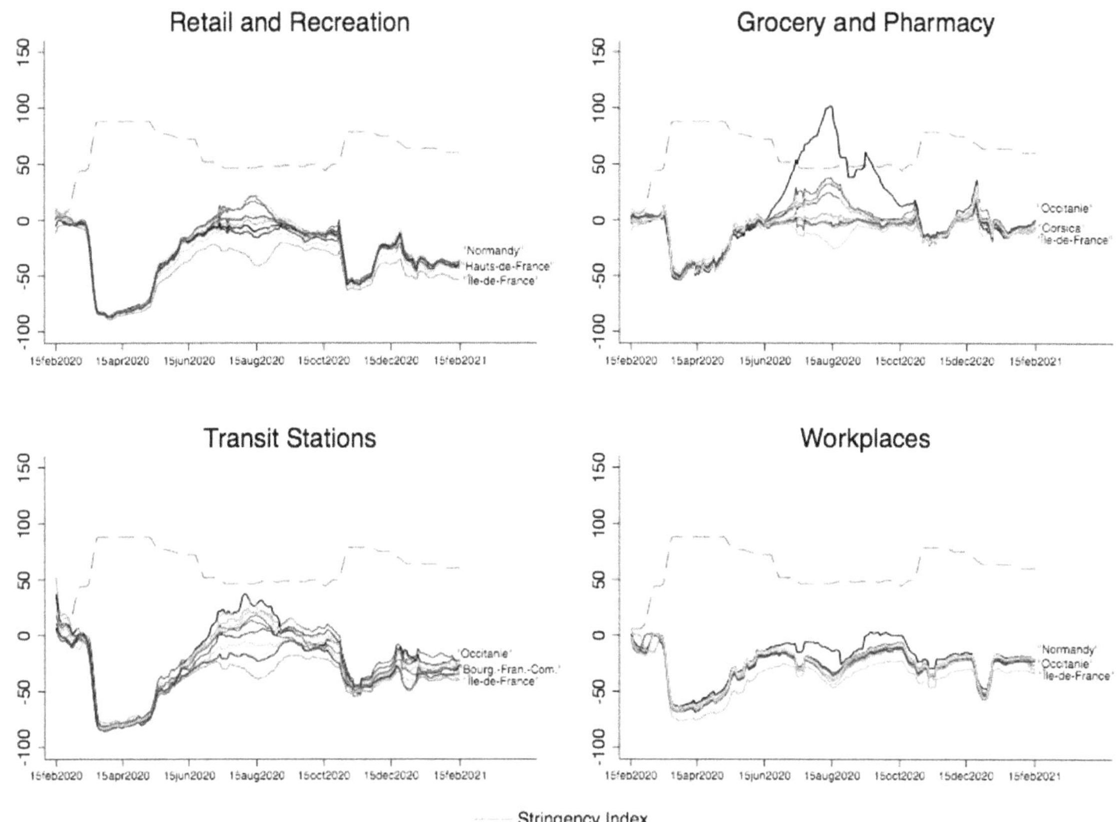

Note: See notes Annex Figure 1.A.7.
Source: Authors' elaboration based on (Google LLC, 2021[3]) and (Hale, T., S. Webster, A. Petherick, T. Phillips, and B. Kira, 2020a[5]).

Annex Figure 1.A.4. Mobility in TL2 regions and Strictness of lockdown policies, Germany

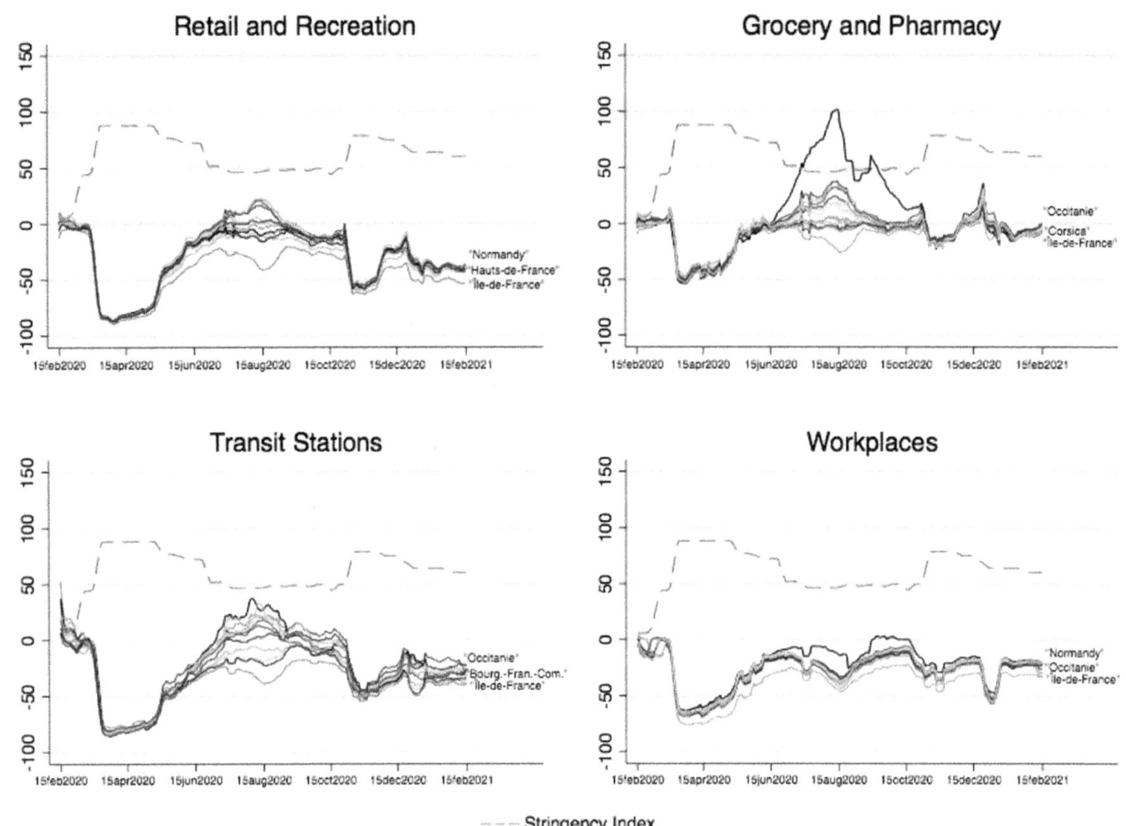

Note: See notes Annex Figure 1.A.7.
Source: Authors' elaboration based on (Google LLC, 2021[3]) and (Hale, T., S. Webster, A. Petherick, T. Phillips, and B. Kira, 2020a[5]).

Annex Figure 1.A.5. Mobility in TL2 regions and Strictness of lockdown policies, Italy

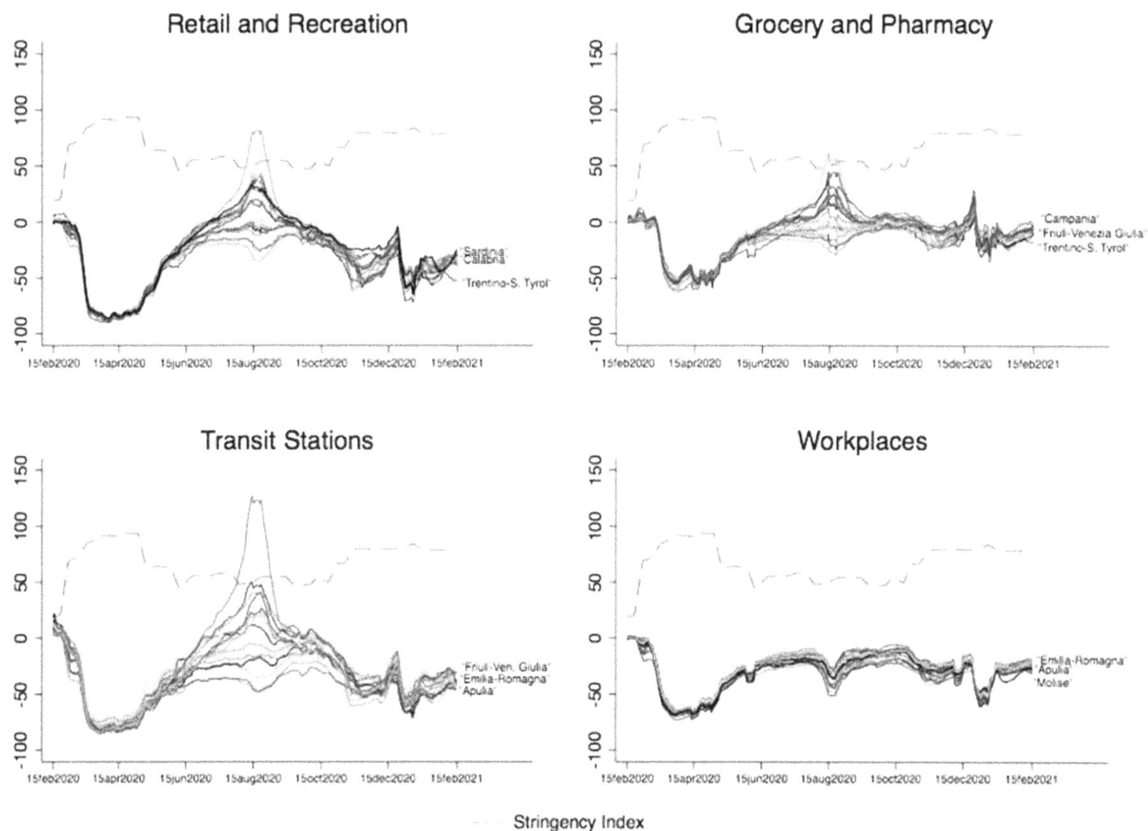

Note: See notes Annex Figure 1.A.7.
Source: Authors' elaboration based on (Google LLC, 2021[3]) and (Hale, T., S. Webster, A. Petherick, T. Phillips, and B. Kira, 2020a[5]).

Annex Figure 1.A.6. Mobility in TL2 regions and Strictness of lockdown policies, Japan

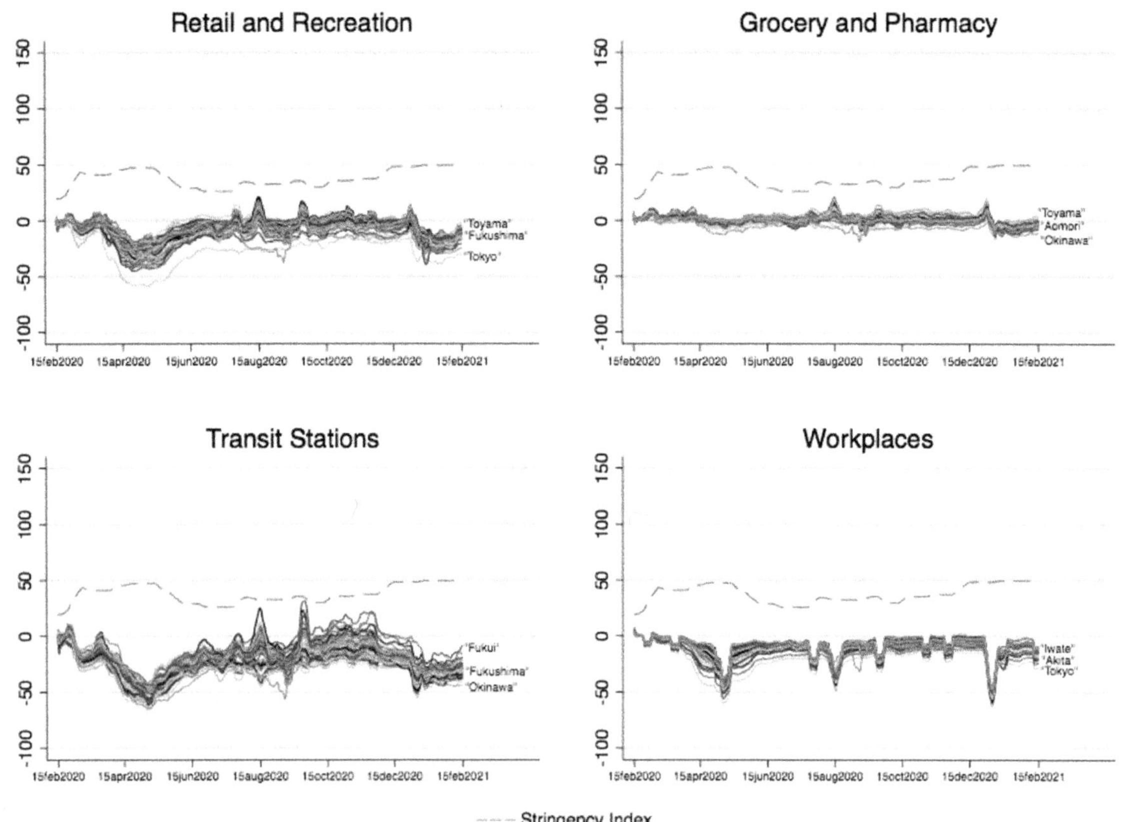

Note: See notes Annex Figure 1.A.7.
Source: Authors' elaboration based on (Google LLC, 2021[3]) and (Hale, T., S. Webster, A. Petherick, T. Phillips, and B. Kira, 2020a[5]).

Annex Figure 1.A.7. Mobility in TL2 regions and Strictness of lockdown policies, United States

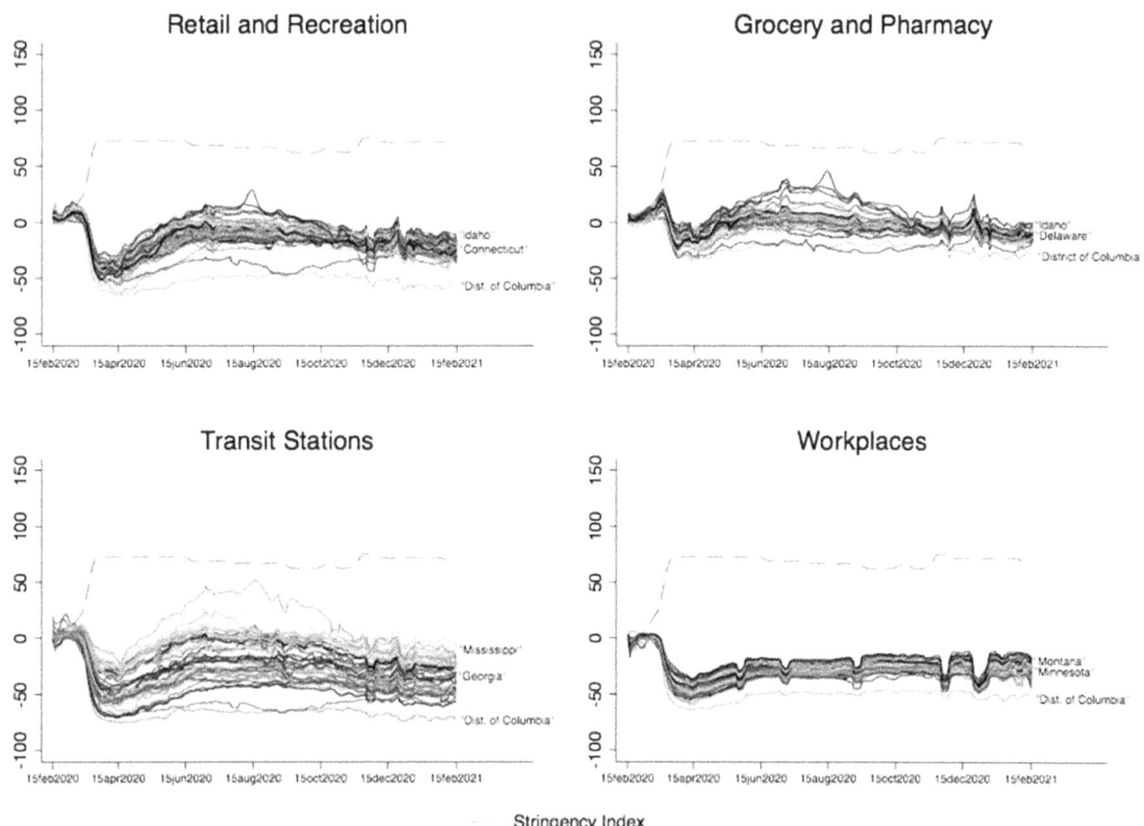

Note: Mobility values correspond to the average of the fortnight's means in the percentage change in mobility (from the median value for the corresponding day of the week from 3 January 2020 to 3 February) to different places (Retail & Recreation, Grocery & Pharmacy, Transit Stations and Workplaces). The stringency index (dosh line) approximates the strictness of the "lockdown style" policies that (primarily) restrict people's behaviour.

Source: Authors' elaboration based on (Google LLC, 2021[3]) and (Hale, T., S. Webster, A. Petherick, T. Phillips, and B. Kira, 2020a[5]).

2 Remote Work and the New Normality

This chapter examines trends in remote working across regions in G7 countries. It starts by setting the scene on permanent movement patterns with evidence from the US. It then presents how remote work is distributed across regions and territories in G7 countries, and the association between characteristics of rural regions and remote working potential. The analysis concludes by emphasising the role of digital infrastructure and female workforce participation in regions' potential for remote work.

The potential for remote working in transforming the workplace is substantial. In some G-7 countries, the COVID-19 crisis has accelerated pre-existing trends in workplace management. In other countries, COVID-19 has introduced new ways of working whereby individuals in occupations with remote work capacity can continue to operate with limited mobility and peer-to-peer interactions on digital platforms.

However, not all jobs are created equal. Task-based requirements that are often linked to the occupational and sectoral characteristic of jobs determine whether or to what extent jobs can thrive in an environment of low mobility. The distribution of such jobs are not necessarily uniform across territories. This chapter will explore some of the socio-economic determinants of remote working, with today's current technological capacities, in regions with varying degrees of rural characteristics.

The analysis in this chapter uses four main sources of data to provide supporting evidence. The first source is the OECD's Regional Database with data capturing regional employment, socio-economic characteristics and basic economic trends from 2000 to 2019. The second source of data pertains to occupational shares extracted from the European Union's Labour Force Survey, the Canadian labour force survey and the American Community Survey. Using the first two sources of data, the estimation method for remote working is based on the method by Dingel and Neiman (2020[1]). Critically, the term "remote working" or "teleworkability" captures the degree to which occupations are amenable to remote work.[1] The third source of data is from the *Ookla for Good* initiative. This data source provides average peak speeds from millions of devices' speed tests, aggregated within grid-level units. The data is further aggregated from the spatial grid levels into TL3 units. Finally, it is aggregated with a classification based on each region's access to cities incorporating density and distance in assigning territorial characteristics to regions, as elaborated in Fadic et al. (2019[2]). The final source of data are monthly counts of permanent official relocations filed at the United States Postal Service for the US case study.[2]

Permanent movement to non-metropolitan regions

The impact of the territorial dimension of the current COVID-19 crisis, which imposed daily physical barriers to mobility and created incentives to consider moving away from the location of work, is currently being debated. In a recent commentary, Ramani and Bloom (2021[3]) used data on listed purchasing prices of houses and the rental market to argue that in the US, the COVID-19 crisis has increased the demand for houses outside of large metropolitan areas. However, they find that this effect is limited to major metropolitan areas and does not necessarily apply to all metropolitan areas. Their analysis of housing prices suggests that the trend is long term.

Following lockdown orders and wider remote working practices, people moved into metropolitan regions at a slower pace and relocations to non-metropolitan regions became more volatile (Figure 2.1, Panel A and B). In the immediate months following lockdown orders, net inflow rates dropped in all areas (Panel A). When adjusted for seasonal trends (Panel B), there was relatively higher net inflow to non-metropolitan areas with access to medium- and small-sized cities (April-June). This may have been due to the acceleration of anticipated movement patterns from denser regions, and limited incentives to move to more remote areas or densely-populated regions. However, the trend did not continue to show a clear direction in the following months. Interestingly, we did however observe a marginally lower-than-expected permanent movement to remote regions. As will be discussed in later sections, this may be due to limited framework conditions that are conducive to remote work in the more remote regions.

Whether the change in permanent patterns will fundamentally adjust human settlement patterns remains to be seen. Permanent mobility was impacted following the lockdown orders and the move to remote working. Like in the "doughnut" hypothesis proposed by some researchers (Bloom and Ramani, 2021[3]), where individuals will expand to the immediate periphery of metropolitan areas, some movement to less populated areas—around the time period when stay-at-home orders were taking effect—is also observable on a more aggregate level. However, at least in the US, permanent settlement patterns in larger functional areas may not be as drastically impacted as is observed in the demand market for housing

(Figure 2.1). Using United States Postal Service data for permanent move requests, we can observe a relative decline in the count of inward mobility in metropolitan areas (Panel A). Once we adjust for monthly (and implicitly, seasonal) trends using average monthly observations for the two prior years, we observe a more normalised trend after the period of the first stay-at-home orders in March (Panel B).

Permanent settlement patterns will continue to evolve as direct impacts and spillover effects on local economies change due to remote working. Currently, there is no clear and dominating consensus of COVID-19's impact on permanent changes to human movement patterns in international policy discourse. However, the current, short-term changes are suggesting that there are direct effects on jobs in occupations that were able to adapt to remote working (Dingel and Neiman, 2020[1]) and indirect effects on jobs that support and provide services to occupations that are better suited to remote work (Althoff et al., 2020[4]). Governments should prepare for territorial changes in demographic patterns of workers including, in particular, fiscal place-based policies and property taxes. However, they should keep in mind that the current territorial distribution of populations is unlikely to change dramatically in the short to medium term, in the recovery period.

Figure 2.1. Net Inflow of permanent relocation requests, by access to city

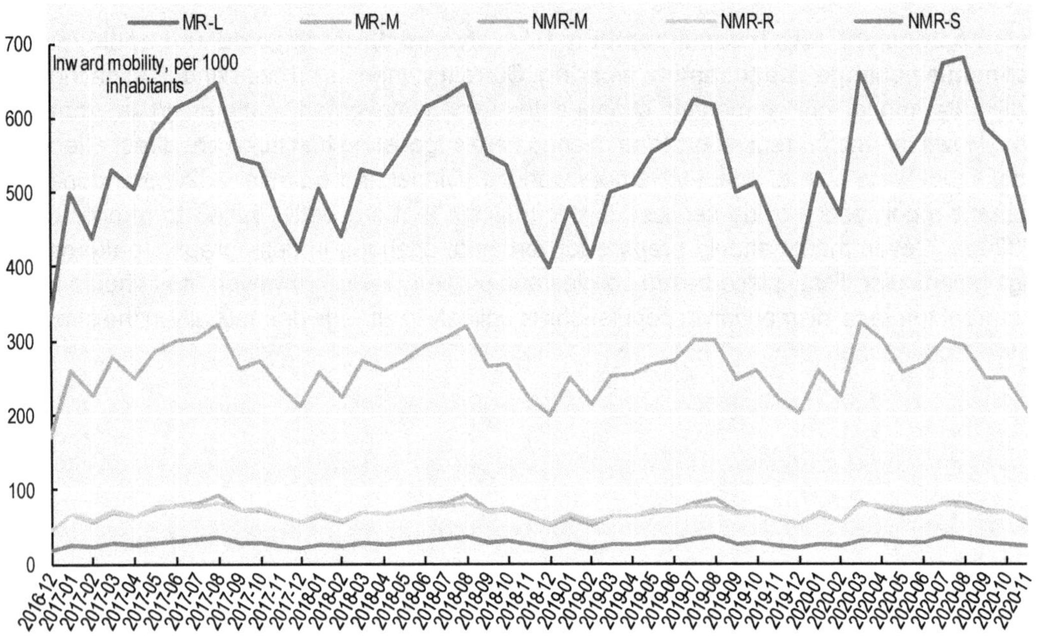

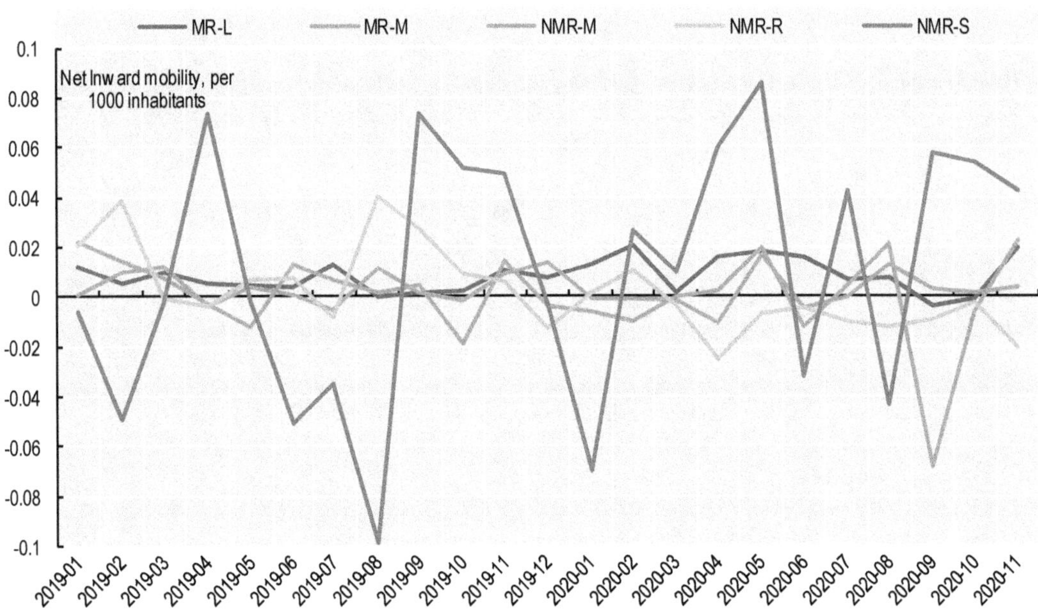

Note: Data reported is the number of registered official requests to move. Adjusted numbers refer to trends adjusted for average movements in previous years.

Source: United States Postal Service

StatLink https://doi.org/10.1787/888934248350 and https://doi.org/10.1787/888934248369

How is remote work distributed across regions?

The suitability of jobs to remote working depends on the type of skills required to carry out occupational tasks. Jobs that can be worked from home have occupational and sectoral characteristics that are often associated with office jobs. For example, tasks in offices, in particular, in sectors such as those in the financial sector or professional services, are more easily conducted from a home office than tasks in physical or labour-intensive occupations in sectors such as the personal service sector, paramedical services sector and hospitality sector. The territorial distribution of such occupations and sectors therefore is an important determinant of how well regions can adapt to the new normality with more widespread remote working arrangements.

Rural regions systematically have lower shares of remote working jobs. In Figure 2.2, most G-7 countries have close to one-third of occupations that are considered easily amenable to remote working. The figure reports higher shares of occupations that can be adapted to remote working in regions with more urban characteristics. Among G-7 countries with available data, the UK has the highest share of remote work occupations, while Canada has the lowest share, followed closely behind by the US.[3]

The disparity between territories within most countries are considerable (Figure 2.2**).** The disparity between regional remote working rates within each country is the largest in France and Italy, and relatively lower in the United Kingdomand Germany. The two countries with the least regional inequality in remote working also have intermediate regions with similar shares of remote work occupations to urban regions. A combination of low regional inequalities in jobs amenable to remote work and relatively advanced intermediate categories suggests a more equal distribution of occupations across regions in United Kingdom and Germany. With a relatively equal territorial distribution of remote work occupations, we can also expect less territorial variability in potential outcomes associated with initiatives to encourage further adoption of a generalised remote work model of human resource management.

Figure 2.2. Remote working in G-7 Countries (2019)

Share of occupations amenable for remote work in TL2 regions, with varying degrees of rurality.

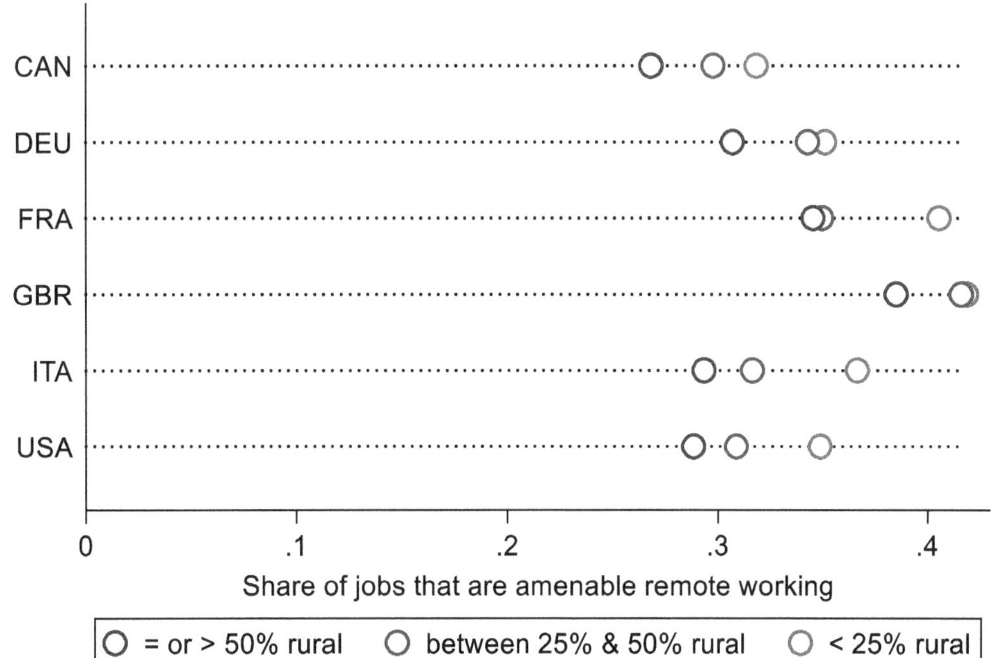

Note: Remote work or teleworkability is estimated following the method by Dingel and Neiman (2020[1]) using labour force surveys in Europe, the US and Canada. It captures the relative share of occupations that are amenable to remote work. The degree of rurality is estimated based on the methodology elaborated by Fadic et al. (2019[2]) using the OECD Regional Database. The methodology for the 5-tiered classification of regions consists in identifying metropolitan and non-metropolitan areas based on percentages of population within each TL3 region that has access to functional urban areas within a 60-minute drive above or below population thresholds of 250 000 and 1.5 million. To accommodate for the fact that regional databases are mostly only representative at the TL2 regions, we generate a continuous variable ranging from 0 to 1 that identifies the percentage of the population within each TL2 region that lives in one of the 3 kinds of TL3 regions identified as non-metropolitan. The first category "= or > 50% rural" refers to TL2 regions that have at least 50% or more of the population identified as living in a TL3 non-metropolitan region. The second category "between 25% & 50% rural" capture regions that have 25% to 50% of the population identified as living in a TL3 non-metropolitan region. The last category "< 25% rural" refer to TL2 regions with less than 25% of the population identified as living in a TL3 non-metropolitan region.

Source: European Labour Forces Survey (2019); American Community Survey (2019); Canadian Labour Force Survey (2020) ; OECD Regional Database

Characteristics of rural regions and remote working

The extent to which an employee can work from home depends on a variety of factors, such as whether a specific physical environment, tools, or physical proximity to colleagues are required for the role. For the rest of the chapter, we only consider the first category of jobs that are suitable to remote working (those whose tasks facilitate it). We also cover other factors such as national regulation and firm management decisions in Chapter 4.

Because most remote work jobs still require collaborative working, the primary factor determining the demand for remote work jobs is access to digital infrastructure. On the other hand, the supply of workers who have skills for occupations where remote working is possible is determined by socio-economic characteristics. The following section analyses access to digital infrastructure, as a key determinant to remote working rates. It follows with sections analysing socio-economic characteristics such as gender, age and education.

Access to Digital Infrastructure

Equal and ubiquitous access to telecommunications infrastructure is an important precondition for reducing territorial inequalities and ensuring that policies are focused on rural well-being (OECD, 2021[5]). Equal access to digital (telecommunication) infrastructure is also within the scope of the recently updated *Recommendation of the Council on Broadband Connectivity* (OECD, 2021[6]), which recommends that Member States take measures to eliminate digital divides and reduce barriers to broadband deployment.

Broadband access is critical for remote working. Figure 2.3 depicts the marginal effects[4] of broadband access, as measured by the share of households with access to internet. Because of the nature of remote working, household access to internet is of keen interest to policy-makers. The figure shows a positive association between broadband access and remote working across all G-7 countries. The level and range of the marginal effects of broadband access on remote working does not vary substantially, suggesting relative stability in this finding.

Figure 2.3. Digital Infrastructure matters for all regions

Average Marginal Effects of Broadband Access (2019)

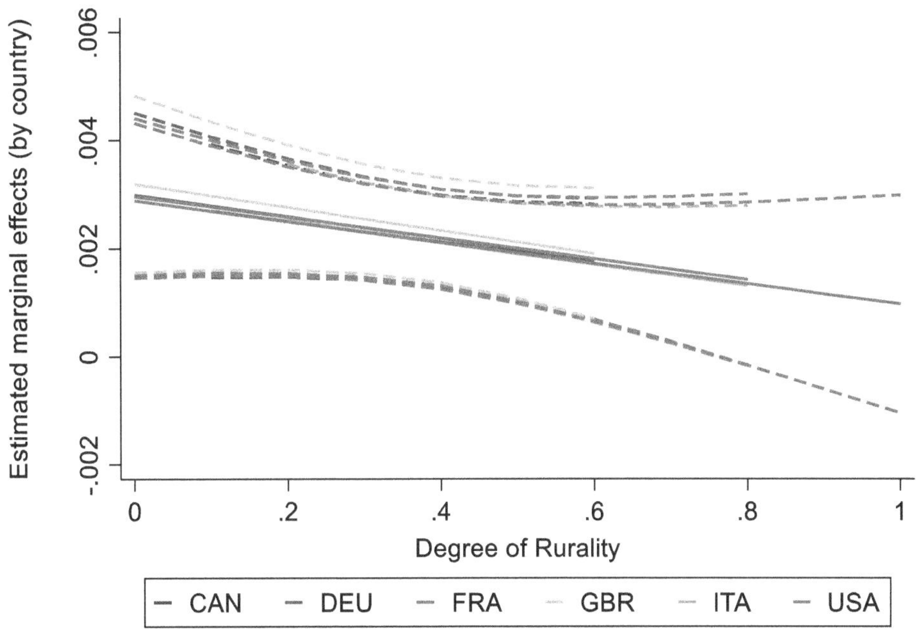

Note: The figure depicts the estimated marginal effects of broadband access on remote working rates with varying degrees of rurality for each of the G-7 countries. The solid lines depict estimates. Dotted lines depict 95% confidence intervals.
Source: EULFS (2019), ACS, CLFS, Fadic et al. (2019[2]), OECD Regional Indicators.

Broadband access matters for all regions, but given the current distribution of occupations, it matters more for urban regions than rural regions. The marginal change associated with one more unit of broadband access in Figure 2.3 is positive across all territories, but downward sloping. This means that broadband access is important for occupations that are amenable to remote work, but as we look to regions with more rural characteristics, we observe that broadband has less explanatory power for explaning trends in remote working potential. For the regions with the highest degree of rurality (over 80%), the marginal effect of broadband access is still positive, but not statistically significant.

The lack of quality broadband may be limiting remote work opportunities in rural regions. While a first level analysis might conclude that broadband is less relevant for rural areas, this is a naïve interpretation. The pre-existence and demand for broadband access is often associated with positive growth in economic activity. Therefore, it is also possible to say that households' lack of broadband access is one of the reasons that certain areas fail to attract remote workers. Indeed, in Figure 2.4, we observe unequal opportunities for areas with a higher degree of rural characteristics. Internet quality, as measured by average peak download speeds on fixed broadband from Ookla, systematically lags behind in non-metropolitan regions. Fixed broadband access and quality produces network effects that influence the structure of regional economies. If broadband access and quality were the same across regions, and the marginal effects of broadband access was still negative sloping, then we could say that the needs of individuals in rural areas are simply different. However, this is not the case. Internet download speeds are systematically lagging behind in non-metropolitan regions. Although they have risen over the first three quarters of 2020 (prior to generalised lockdown measures) in most countries, the increase have not lead to reductions in the gap between rural and urban regions.

In countries where there is a more equitable distribution (low variance) of internet speeds between territories, there was also a more equitable distribution in the shares of remote working jobs. Both the UK and Germany have low variance of remote working jobs (Figure 2.2) and more equal internet download speeds across types of territories (Figure 2.4). Countries like France and the US have the highest levels of differences between different types of territories, even if they both also simultaneously have the relatively high speeds in the largest metropolitan regions. This polarity is also reflected in the fact that intermediate territorial categories have lower shares of remote working occupations as compared to metropolitan regions.

Figure 2.4. Fixed Broadband Download Speeds (2020, Q1-Q4)

Deviation of average download speed in fixed broadband (mbps) from country average (weighted mean), 2020

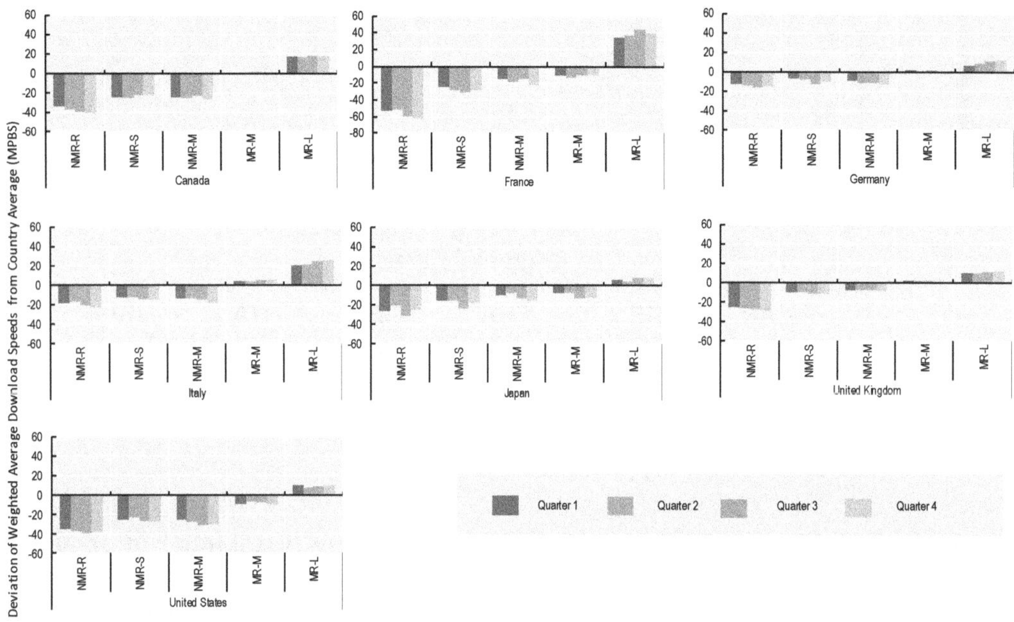

Note: The data for average fixed broadband download Speedtests reported by Ookla measures the sustained peak throughput achieved by users of the network. Measurements are based on self-administered tests by users, carried over iOS and mobile devices. The values capture the average peak speeds, rather than absolute peak speeds and may not align perfectly with sources such as m-labs or steam due to differences in measurement methodology. The figure presents the deviation (in levels) from the average peak speeds observed in the country. Territorial aggregation according to the OECD typology based on access to cities is available from Fadic et al. 2019. The figure presents the deviation of average peak speed tests (weighted by the number of tests) from country means. For further information on the degree of urbanisation, the definition and treatment of the Speedtest data, please see OECD (forthcoming), G-20: Synthesis report on existing digital divides. OECD Publishing : Paris.

StatLink https://doi.org/10.1787/888934248388

Female employment and remote work

Women make up 46% of the active labour force[5] in G-7 countries (OECD, 2020[7]), with a participation rate systematically lower than that of men in all G-7 countries (Figure 2.5). Within G-7 countries, the largest differences between female and male labour force participation rates are in Italy[6], while the lowest differences are in Canada. Rurality alone does not determine the rates of female participation, but it is one component of occupational composition that governments need to consider when shaping policy that will facilitate the transition to the new normal. The variation of women in the workforce in regions with different degrees of rurality is an important determinant of the capacity of regional economies to adopt remote work in response to the pandemic.

Figure 2.5. Average gap in female participation rate

Female - Male, 2019

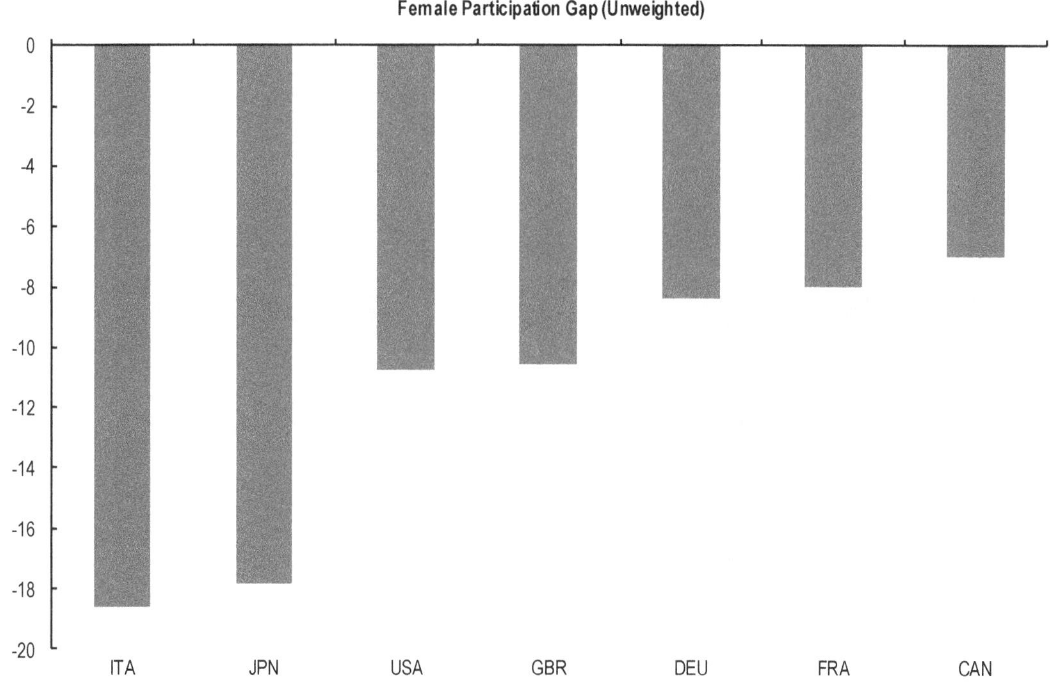

Note: The participation rate is the ratio of the working-age population (15-64) that is active in the labour force (whether they are employed, looking for work, or in training), over the total working-age population. Graph depicts regional averages of the difference between female and male participation rates.
Source: OECD Regional Indicators, ACS, CLFS

StatLink https://doi.org/10.1787/888934248407

On average, more women tend to have occupations amenable to remote work than men. In Figure 2.6, the marginal effects of a higher level of participation in private sector employment of females on remote work is generally positive and upward sloping across degrees of rurality. However, it is important to note that female participation trends are not the same across all sectors and occupations. For example, women tend to be over-represented in the public sector both in critical, non-general services (e.g., health care sector) that were ill-suited to remote work. However, this was also the case for the education sector, which did have to largely transition to remote work during the crisis (OECD, 2017[8]; OECD, 2020[9]). In all G-7 countries, except for Japan, women filled more than 50% of public sector jobs. As such, the spatial clustering of public sector jobs will tend to correlate with both higher levels of female employment and, in some cases, remote working. In addition, while the average woman may have a job that is more amenable to remote work, such positions are likely middle management and secretarial occupations, as women are still under-represented in senior management positions (OECD, 2017[8]), and more exposed to part-time and precarious work (OECD, 2020[9]).

In addition, women in rural regions tend to have jobs more amenable to remote working than in denser areas. In fact, regions with higher than 25% of the population living in an area characterised as rural see a statistically significant impact of having higher rates of female employment on remote working. This is a clear avenue for governments looking to attain dual goals of more remote working and equality in the workforce. Encouraging a culture of where remote work is more acceptable for those who need flexibility, while simultaneously focusing on work-life balance provisions are key recommendations to help reduce gender gaps in the workforce, during and after the COVID-19 crisis. For rural areas, this also means placing more focus on childcare arrangements for women who are less likely to work from home due to the task-based nature of their jobs.

Figure 2.6. Average marginal effects of female labour force participation rate on remote working rates

Female Participation Rate (15-64 years old)

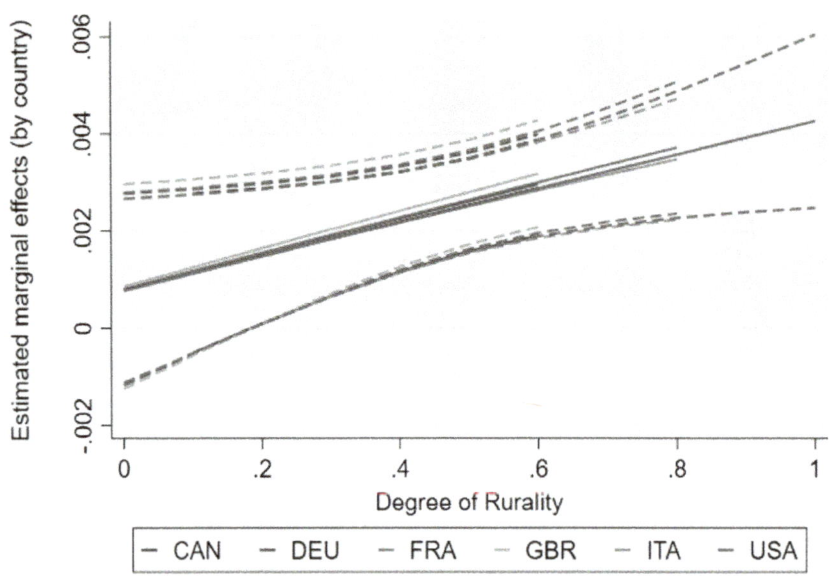

Note: Female participation rate refers to active labour force between the ages of 15 and 64 that are female, within each TL2 region.
Source: EULFS (2019), ACS, CLFS, Fadic et al. (2019[2]), OECD Regional Indicators

The wider implementation of remote working has the potential to substantially affect intra-household decision-making. Prior to the crisis, remote working arrangements were often considered to be part of work-life balance initiatives, often through labour regulations or collective bargaining that established better working conditions through flexibility around provisions for maternity, paternity, parental leave, as well as childcare, dependent parents or sick family member leave (OECD, 2012[10]). However, with mandated remote working, and school closures, these measures no longer provide the relief needed for balancing work-life obligations, as they did prior to the crisis. For example, during the pandemic, preliminary findings suggest that due to government measures, households in the UK increased time spent on childcare by about 40 hours, or a whole additional work week, with a larger share of the work conducted by women. The study did however also find that childcare duties were reallocated within the household when men were furloughed or lost employment (Sevilla and Smith, 2020[11]). Findings were similar in regards to the intra-household share of domestic workloads in the UK (Amuedo-Dorantes et al., 2020[12]).Going into the new normality, governments should consider how increased remote working may inadvertently create disadvantages for the female labour force. While the pre-existing legal framework for remote working in most OECD countries focused on helping women (and primary care takers) remain in the labour market, the current implementation of a wider, and more generalized remote working scheme may create additional challenges.

A few key recommendations for helping women in adapting to a generalised remote working scenario should include implementing policies such as prioritising public childcare options and subsidising alternatives, direct financial support for female workers who take leave due to childcare responsibilities, providing financial incentives for employers who provide workers with paid leave, and promoting flexibility in remote working (OECD, 2012[10]; OECD, 2020[13]; OECD, 2020[14]). In addition, because access to public facilities for childcare are often more difficult for women in rural regions, special focus on alternative arrangements and flexibility at the workplace is increasingly important for women in rural regions. Age-based differences in remote working trends

Remote working creates new opportunities for older workers and workers living in rural areas that may prefer (or need) to live closer to nature. The age-based demographic distribution across regions is well documented (OECD, 2021[5]), and implies that special focus should be placed on policies that focus on age demographics in different territories.

The geographical divide is also a generational divide. On a very basic level, Figure 2.7 demonstrates that as territories become more characterized by rural attributes, the share of older working age population (50-64) increases, while the share of the younger working population (15-29) decreases. In areas with the highest degree of rurality, the older working age population makes up 53% of the population, while the younger share of the population makes up 17% of the population. In the most densely populated areas, the older working age population makes up 49% of the population, while the young working age population makes up to 25% of the total population. The increase in the share of older and younger demographic groups in regions with higher rural characteristics makes the demographic composition of economies important when considering policies and programmes to adjust to a new normality and remote working.

Figure 2.7. The Territorial generational divide among older and younger working age populations

Share of young working age population, and share of older worker age populations in TL2 regions and degree of rurality.

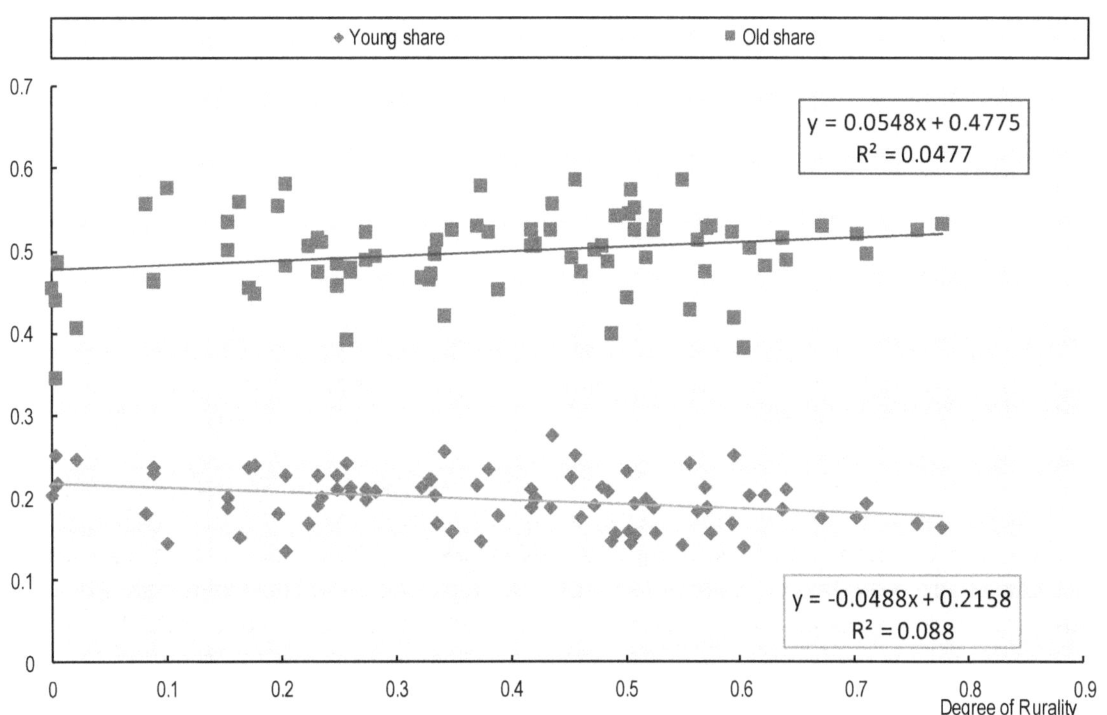

Note: Young share is the share of 15-29 year olds in the population, over individuals 15 years old and older. Old share is the share of 50-64 year olds, over the 15 + population.
Source: OECD Regional Database

StatLink https://doi.org/10.1787/888934248426

The transition to remote work improves opportunities for youth in rural regions and the attractiveness of rural areas for retaining youth. As depicted in Figure 2.8, there is a positive association between the young working age population and the share of jobs amenable to remote working. Increasing remote work opportunities may help alleviate the depopulation trends in less urbanised areas, and improve the attractiveness of regions to younger residents.

Figure 2.8. Inter-generational dependencies and remote work in 2019

Share of jobs amenable to remote work, young working age to population ratios and elderly dependency ratios in TL2 regions.

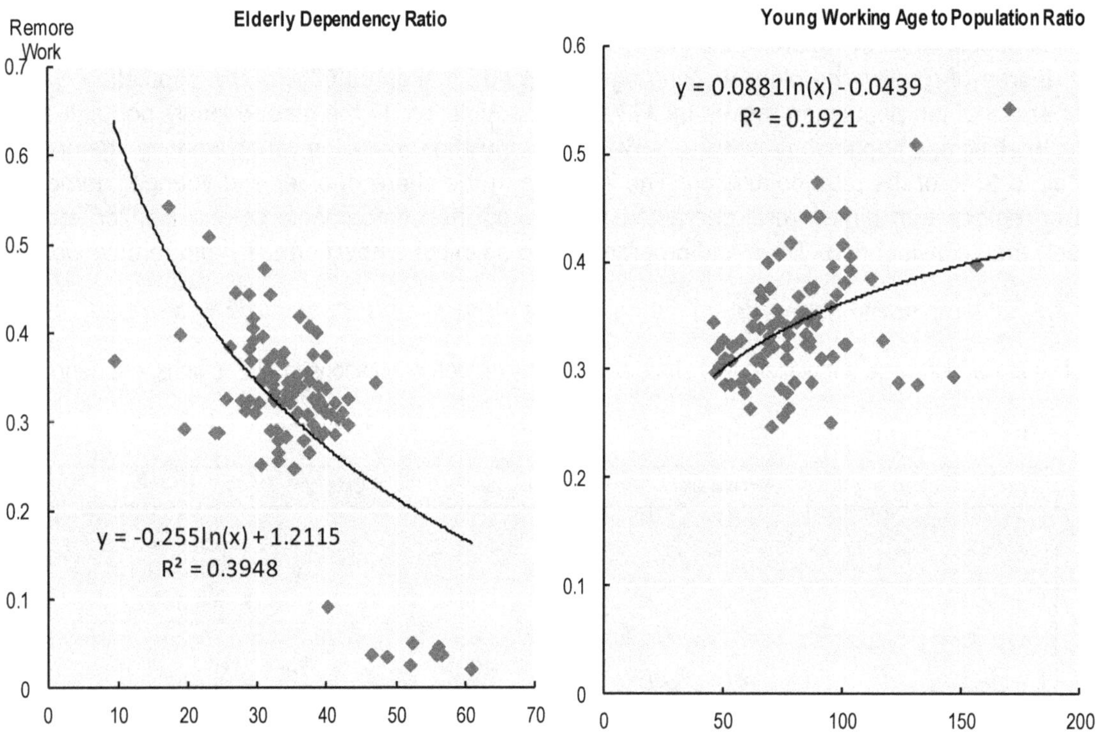

Note: Young working age to population ratio is the ratio of working age youth between the ages of 15 and 29 to the population above 15 years of age. The graph excludes the US and Japan due to data availability. The elderly dependency ratio is the ratio of older population (65+) to the working age population (15 – 64). It excludes the US due to data availability. In the graph on young working age to population ratio above, region French Guiana (FRY3) is excluded as an outlier.

StatLink https://doi.org/10.1787/888934248445

The relationship between remote working and older workers (50-64) depends on how well older workers can adapt to digital communication tools. Currently, the trend between remote working rates and older workers is unclear on an aggregate level. The ratio of older working age population to the rest of the population did not show any conclusive trends (not depicted). One explanation for this could be related to two concurrent and opposing trends in occupational characteristics related to remote work, seniority and technical skills. Over the trajectory of careers, workers increase seniority with age, and find themselves in more managerial positions. Managerial positions, in turn, are among the occupational categories that have the highest rates of potential remote work. In the opposite direction, older workers have had relatively less exposure to digital occupations and skills development than relatively younger workers, making their work less amenable to remote work. Understanding what types of skills are required for workers in the later stages of their career is an important aspect to consider when designing place-based policies.

Remote work arrangements create more opportunities for providing services to elderly demographics. The adoption of a generalised remote work model has the potential to make work arrangements and services better suited to the needs of older individuals with less mobility. In Figure 2.8, we observe that areas with a relatively high-level of old age dependency ratios (65+) also have low remote work potential, leaving an opportunity for tele-services to improve the quality of life for older demographics. When working-from-home becomes more widespread, elderly populations can gain access to otherwise unavailable services. The variation in remote work is partly due to territorial distribution of occupations. Jobs that focus on the needs and welfare of the elderly are often in the service, health and community sectors. However, many jobs with face-to-face and physical proximity requirements in particular for the health sector, are often incompatible with remote work unless such occupations can harness technologies to adapt and overcome digital privacy and security barriers, and transition to providing *high quality* services via digital platforms. For this purpose, special attention should be paid to continuing to provide basic public services to elderly populations while developing digital solutions that may help the elderly population to continue to receive quality healthcare and community services.

Education and remote work occupations

Education plays an important role in preparing workers for occupations that are amenable to remote work. To begin with, education creates a supply of skilled workers who are trained for occupations with remote work aspects. Following this, the opportunity to remote work for these skilled workers means that workers with a preference for living in different regions may now have more liberty to move in a more permanent way.

Rural regions have a lower share of the labour force with tertiary education. The depopulation of many rural regions is, in part, lead by the loss of younger workers who leave to pursue higher levels of education, as well as those seeking the amenities and opportunities that arise with agglomeration economies in denser regions. As demonstrated for G-7 countries in Panel A of Figure 2.9, the relationship between education and rurality is not perfectly linear, or precise; however, the trend shows that areas with increasingly rural characteristics also have a relatively larger share of primary and secondary workers, and a relatively lower share of tertiary workers.

Regions with high shares in both tertiary and primary educated workers tend to also have a high share of occupations amenable to remote work (Figure 2.9, Panel B). It is clear that where there are higher shares of tertiary educated workers, regions also tend to have a high share of occupations amenable to remote work in OECD countries (OECD, 2020[15]). In G-7 countries, the trend for tertiary workers is similar. Simultaneously, regions with high shares of occupations amenable to remote work are often supported by a high-degree of local service sector jobs (e.g. food and delivery services, healthcare). When regional employment consists of a large share of occupations that can be worked remotely, they are often supported by occupations that require less education, that often are at the lower end of the income distribution, creating a dichotomy of occupations within regions. Policies need to concurrently consider how to support an economy with both high-educated, high-paid workers who can work remotely, and the lower-educated, low-wage workers who provide support to these workers.

The new normality is worrisome for middle-skilled workers in rural regions. In Figure 2.9, as regions increasingly have rural characteristics, the share of secondary workers also increases. However, the relationship between the share of middle-educated workers and remote work goes in the opposite direction. Regions that have increasing shares of middle-educated workers tend to have a lower share of remote work occupations. A new normality with mass remote working is not as suitable for workers with a secondary level of education, as it is for highly educated workers, and the increasing share of such secondary educated workers in rural regions is an economic and well-being challenge for governments.

Figure 2.9. G-7 regions with highly educated workers are more often in dense areas

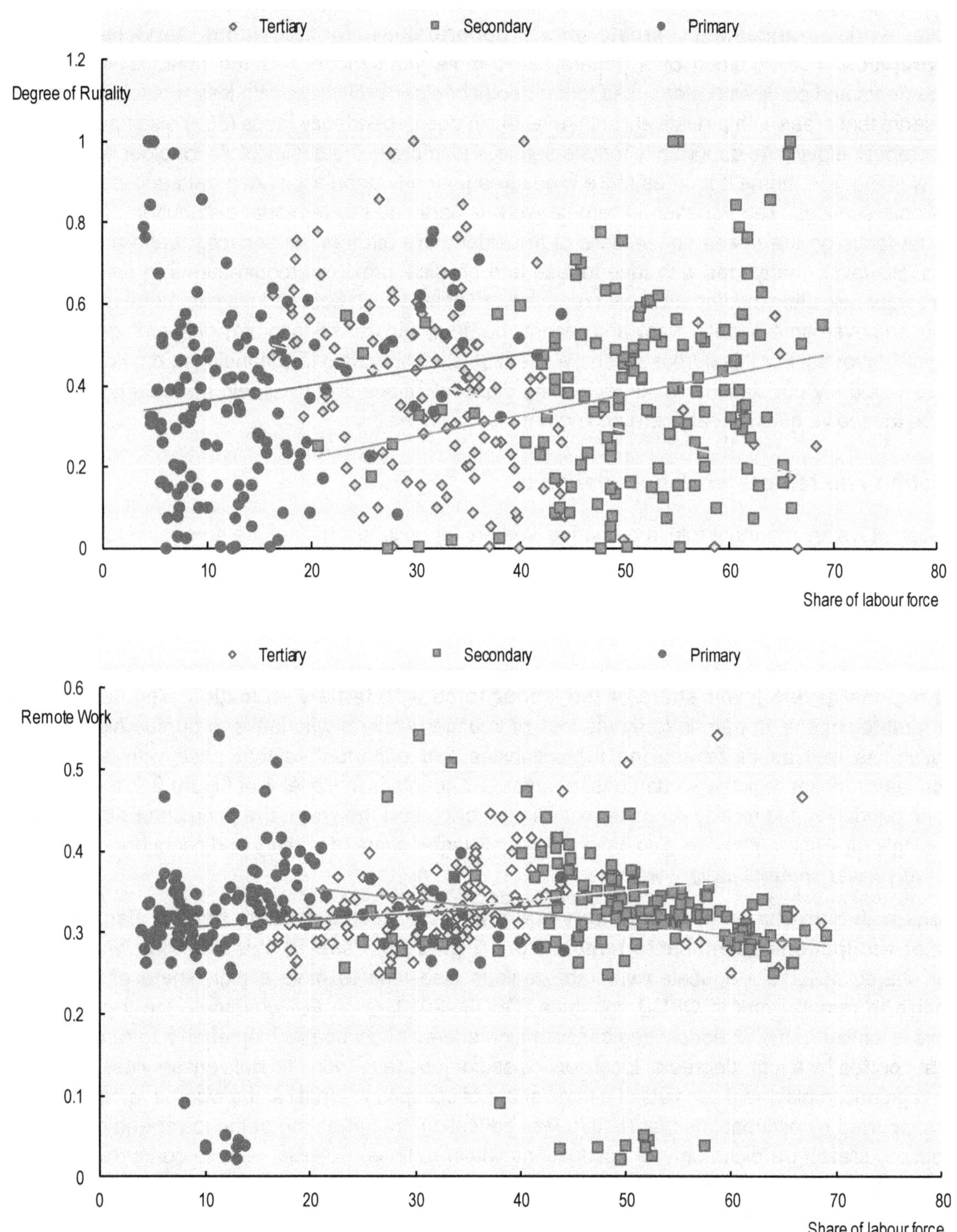

Note: Includes only G-7 countries with available data.
Source: OECD Regional Indicators.

StatLink https://doi.org/10.1787/888934248464

The remote work potential in regions

Understanding the characteristics of regions with varying degrees of rurality is an important aspect of understanding the COVID-related after-shocks. How policies adapt to the new normality impacts regions differently. Governments wishing to pursue strategies encouraging widespread remote work as part of a new normality need to take into consideration the distribution of workers across regions.

The conclusions from the analysis in the previous sections can be summarised as follows:

- There is no current consensus of the permanence of territorial relocation due to COVID; however, generalised remote working may impact where individuals choose to live in the longer term.
- The distribution of remote work occupations varies across regions. There are fewer jobs that are amenable to remote work in regions that are characterised by higher levels of rurality.
- Access to digital infrastructure is important for remote working arrangements in all regions, but currently it matters more for more densely populated regions with a higher share of remote work occupations. This is likely impacted by lack of access to digital infrastructure.
- Access to high-speed digital infrastructure is systematically lacking in rural regions. The lack of digital infrastructure is likely impacting territorial remote work potential.
- Women's jobs are positively correlated with remote work, but a generalised transition to remote work may also have adverse intra-household impacts depending on the level of support available for working women.
- There is a generational divide across territories in rural regions. Younger workers (15-29) may participate more in remote work, but outcomes for older workers (50-64) depend on whether they are able to transition to jobs that require digital skills, and outcomes for the elderly depend on whether they continue to receive *quality* public services.
- More ubiquitous remote working has the potential to exacerbate inequalities between workers in regions. Non-metropolitan regions (rural regions) have a lower share of tertiary educated workers. Because tertiary workers are more likely to hold positions that are better suited to remote work, this means that rural regions may struggle to attract employment amenable to working from home. On the other hand, there is also a high share of primary educated workers working in support services jobs in metropolitan regions where jobs are highly amenable to remote work.
- The most precarious types of workers in non-metropolitan (rural) regions are those with secondary level of education, who are less likely to have jobs amenable to remote work and more likely to represent the highest share of workers in non-metropolitan (rural) regions.

Taking all of the aforementioned relevant aspects of regional socio-economic characteristics, there are two strong messages that stand out in particular for G-7 countries, the participation rate of females, and access to telecommunications infrastructure (Figure 2.10). Additionally, further analysis is needed to understand occupational trends for men and foreign workers.

Figure 2.10. Access to digital infrastructure and women's participation in the labour force are key regional indicators of remote work

Regression analysis on the potential for remote work at the TL2 level (2019)

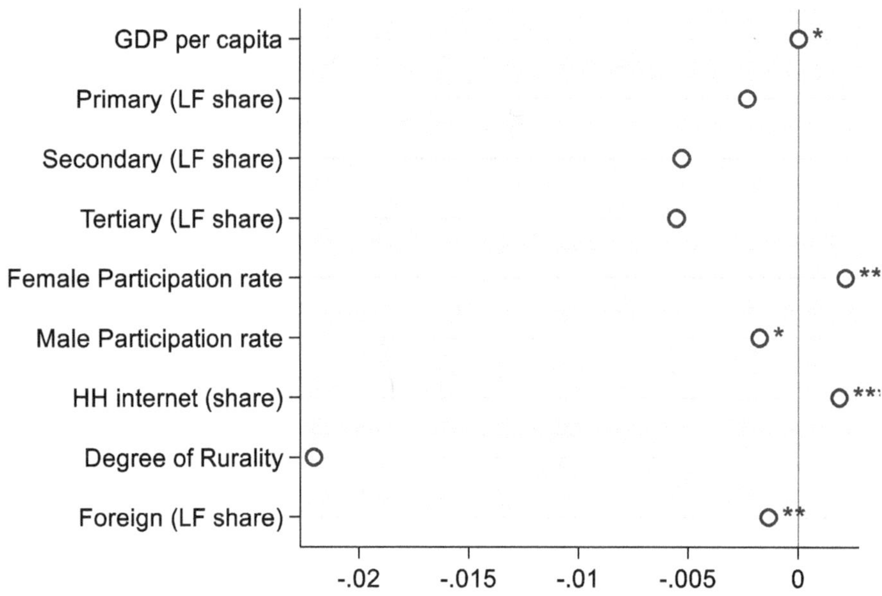

Note: Analysis includes Canada, France, Germany, Italy, the US and UK. Japan was excluded due to limited access to occupational data to provide comparative remote work estimates. The reported estimation is from a linear regression model including additional controls for sectoral gross domestic product and capital regions.
Source: EULFS, CLFS, ACS

Women are more likely to have jobs amenable to remote work, yet in non-metropolitan (rural) regions there is a lower female participation rate than in metropolitan regions. Taking the fact that women tend to have more remote work jobs than men, and the lower rate of female participation in rural areas, generalised remote work arrangements create an implicit opportunity for rural recovery through female employment. The current lag in participation rates in some G-7 countries creates the impetus to both expand practices that incorporate the new normality, while simultaneously improving the labour market outcomes of women. However, governments need to carefully consider how to elaborate regulations and encourage practices in firms that support work-life balance of women entering the workforce, in jobs that have a remote working potential.

Access to quality digital infrastructure is systematically lower in rural areas, creating a primordial challenge for G-7 governments to overcome as they transition to the new normality. The most dominant factor that helps regions encourage remote work is access to telecommunications infrastructure. Investing in telecommunications and understanding policy solutions that provide ubiquitous access to high-speed internet should be the top priority of governments. As we have seen in the past, with regard to regulations related to the expansion of telecommunications infrastructure (OECD, 2021[5]), and as we have seen more recently in several of the Covid-19 related government interventions further explored in Chapter 4, expanding telecommunications access does not *de facto* lead to equal access to remote jobs across regions. Governments should focus on ensuring quality access, which is an issue that is rarely resolved by competition policy alone.

References

Althoff, L. et al. (2020), "The City Paradox: Skilled Services and Remote Work", *CESifo Working Paper No. 8734*, https://www.cesifo.org/en/wp. [4]

Amuedo-Dorantes, C. et al. (2020), *COVID-19 School Closures and Parental Labor Supply in the United States*, https://www.iza.org/publications/dp/13827/covid-19-school-closures-and-parental-labor-supply-in-the-united-states (accessed on 11 May 2021). [12]

Bloom, N. and A. Ramani (2021), *The donut effect: How COVID-19 shapes real estate*, https://siepr.stanford.edu/sites/default/files/publications/SIEPR%20Policy%20Brief%20January%202021%20v04.pdf (accessed on 13 March 2021). [3]

Dingel, J. and B. Neiman (2020), "How many jobs can be done at home?", *Journal of Public Economics*, Vol. 189, p. 104235, http://dx.doi.org/10.1016/j.jpubeco.2020.104235. [1]

Fadic, M. et al. (2019), "Classifying small (TL3) regions based on metropolitan population, low density and remoteness", *OECD Regional Development Working Papers*, No. 2019/06, OECD Publishing, Paris, https://dx.doi.org/10.1787/b902cc00-en. [2]

OECD (2021), *Delivering Quality Education and Health Care to All: Preparing Regions for Demographic Change*, OECD Rural Studies, OECD Publishing, Paris, https://dx.doi.org/10.1787/83025c02-en. [5]

OECD (2021), *Recommendation of the Council on Broadband Connectivity, OECD/LEGAL/0322*, https://legalinstruments.oecd.org/en/instruments/OECD-LEGAL-0322 (accessed on 13 March 2021). [6]

OECD (2020), *Capacity for remote working can affect lockdown costs differently across places*, https://www.oecd.org/coronavirus/policy-responses/capacity-for-remote-working-can-affect-lockdown-costs-differently-across-places-0e85740e/#blocknotes-d7e290 (accessed on 3 March 2021). [15]

OECD (2020), *OECD Employment Outlook 2020: Worker Security and the COVID-19 Crisis*, OECD Publishing, Paris, https://dx.doi.org/10.1787/1686c758-en. [9]

OECD (2020), "Evolution of gender gap in employment rate: Americas, 2010-18: Difference between the gender gap (male-female) in 2018 and the gap in 2010, large regions (TL2)", in *OECD Regions and Cities at a Glance 2020*, OECD Publishing, Paris, https://dx.doi.org/10.1787/959d5ba0-en. [7]

OECD (2020), *OECD Regions and Cities at a Glance 2020*, OECD Publishing, Paris, https://dx.doi.org/10.1787/959d5ba0-en. [16]

OECD (2020), *Who Cares? Attracting and Retaining Care Workers for the Elderly*, OECD Health Policy Studies, OECD Publishing, Paris, https://dx.doi.org/10.1787/92c0ef68-en. [13]

OECD (2020), *Women at the core of the fight against COVID-19 crisis*, https://www.oecd.org/coronavirus/policy-responses/women-at-the-core-of-the-fight-against-covid-19-crisis-553a8269 (accessed on 23 February 2021). [14]

OECD (2017), "Women in public sector employment", in *Government at a Glance 2017*, OECD Publishing, Paris, https://dx.doi.org/10.1787/gov_glance-2017-27-en. [8]

OECD (2012), *Closing the Gender Gap: Act Now*, OECD Publishing, Paris, https://dx.doi.org/10.1787/9789264179370-en. [10]

Sevilla, A. and S. Smith (2020), *Baby Steps: The Gender Division of Childcare during the COVID-19 Pandemic*, https://www.iza.org/publications/dp/13302/baby-steps-the-gender-division-of-childcare-during-the-covid-19-pandemic (accessed on 11 May 2021). [11]

Notes

[1] More precisely, the method the authors use is based on text mining for key words associated with advertised occupations. The method captures whether this text reflects work that may be conducted from outside the office or physical location of work.

[2] In the United States, the Census Bureau uses official registers from the United States Postal Service to update official population statistics, however estimates from the Census Bureau are updated on a yearly basis, whereas the USPS data can be obtained on a more frequent basis.

[3] Findings from a preliminary draft report that compared actual remote working to estimated remote working shares found that actual remote working shares were only marginally lower than estimated remote working shares. In the initial stages of government imposed lockdowns, the estimated shares more closely reflected actual remote working rates. As government restrictions were lifted, the shares of individuals that were remote working decreased.

[4] The term "marginal effects" refers to the change associated with one extra unit of change in a related variable. In Figure 2.3, one extra unit (degree) of broadband access is associated with more remote work. However, as we increase the degree of rurality, this association decreases. As such, regions with very few rural characteristics (0 on the x-axis) have a positive association between broadband access and remote work (.002), whereas those with at least 40% of the population in rural areas, have a positive association, but to a lesser extent than regions with no rural population (.001). The dotted lines represent the intervals around which we are confident that our estimates are different than 0. For regions where at least 70% of the population is rural, the confidence intervals (dotted lines) indicate that we can no longer confidently say that estimates are different than 0.

[5] This is calculated as the share of females in the working age labour force (15-64 years of age) in all G-7 countries in 2019.

[6] In the Veneto region, where close to 60% of the population lives outside of a functional urban area, the participation rate of men is much higher than that of women (25.5 point difference). Within the same country, in the Apulia region where close to 50% of the population lives outside of a functional urban area, which is lower than the country average, female participation rates are much lower than those of men (-32 point difference). The unweighted regional average in Italy for the percentage of the labour force living in rural TL3 regions, within TL2 regions is 53%. Overall, regions in Italy have a higher percentage of rural population than other G-7 countries. In comparison, the regional average is 37% in Canada, 43% in France, 23 % in Germany, 32% in Japan, 25% in the UK, and 40% in the US, based on the author's calculations.

3 Labour markets in the new normality

This chapter examines the structural effects of COVID-19 on the labour markets in a set of G7 countries. It starts by presenting evidence on the different workers' potential to shift from presence to remote working amid lockdowns and social distancing measures in Canada, Europe and the U.S. Then, for the United States, it documents the uneven effects of the COVID-crisis across groups of workers in the labour market and the importance of remote work for attenuating the adverse effects during the period. Lastly, it discusses the possible repercussions of the crisis on the inequalities in the labour market in the short and medium run.

Introduction

COVID-19 has ushered in a new normal where remote working is increasingly widespread. To deal with the spread of COVID-19, governments have implemented strict containment measures such as social distancing and stay-at-home policies to deal with the spread of COVID-19. Such measures have required closing many workplaces, with most of the labour force obliged to work from home. In order to adapt to the sudden change of circumstances, firms have undergone a technological transition and reorganisation to allow their workers to operate from home. Thanks to this rapid transformation, some workers were able to continue working remotely, at least partially, sometimes with almost no activity reduction.

Differences in remote working potential can exacerbate existing inequalities. The possibility to keep working remotely while the pandemic containment measures are in place is mainly determined by workers' occupations, which are in turn highly correlated with workers' education or income. This means that some groups of workers (e.g., low-skilled, low-income, female, young, etc.) are less likely to work remotely. In that case, these groups may be hit harder by the economic crisis, further widening already existing inequalities within labour markets. Identifying the specific groups that are more vulnerable to the crisis could help governments develop policies that aim to minimise the income losses in the short run but also help develop medium-run policies that encourage the return of these groups to the labour market and training to equip them with necessary skills allowing them to adapt to the new normal.

This chapter is composed of three sections. The first section provides an assessment of the remote working capacity of workers employed across 31 countries in Europe, Canada and the U.S. to shed light on lockdowns' uneven effect along socio-demographic dimensions. The second section examines the short-term consequences of COVID-19 on employment and wages in the United States. It shows that the labour market effect of COVID-19 has been uneven across different groups. In particular, young, non-white, and less-educated workers suffered sharper increases in their unemployment rates and a more significant decline in working hours and labour force participation. The second section shows that workers who could work remotely were affected less severely than those who cannot. The final section discusses the medium- and long-term implications of the labour market effects of the crisis. It highlights the importance of ensuring an inclusive recovery in the labour market.

Who can work from home?

The COVID-19 pandemic forced many workplaces and most of the workforce to work from home. Governments have implemented strict containment measures and stay-at-home policies to reduce the spread of the virus and the pressure on the health system. As the measures required closing many workplaces, most of the labour force was forced to stay home and start working remotely.

However, not all workers are able to work from home. Due to differences in the nature of each occupation's daily tasks, remote working potential is significantly different across occupations (see Box 3.1 for a detailed explanation). For example, jobs requiring workers to be outdoors (e.g., food delivery person) or to use heavy equipment (e.g., a vehicle) are unlikely to be worked from home. In contrast, occupations requiring only a laptop and an internet connection (e.g., an accountant, finance specialist, etc.) will have a high potential to work remotely. There is a strong positive correlation between the skill level required for an occupation and its remote working potential. Managers, lawyers and I.T. workers are easily adaptable to remote working, in contrast with other occupations such as farmers, construction workers and artisans. Overall, the probability of holding a job requiring a physical presence is higher in specific social groups, such as low-skilled and low-wage workers.

During the pandemic, workers who could work from home faced lower risks of job and income losses. As discussed in the next section, workers who could work remotely were also significantly less likely to report COVID-19 unemployment and work absences. In contrast, workers who had to be physically present were much more likely to report COVID-19 unemployment and absences. The distribution of new job postings reflects similar trends. While the number of job postings decreased dramatically across European capitals during the pandemic, the drop was more tempered for jobs with high remote working potential (Adrjan and Kleine-Rueschkamp, 2021[1]).

Beyond the employment advantages, remote working also helped workers stay healthy. Working from home enabled workers to avoid face-to-face contacts in offices and public transportation, which reduced their probability of contracting the virus (Alipour, Fadinger and Schymik, 2021[2]). Consequently, workers who could work remotely faced lower risks of exposure and COVID-19 infection risk compared to those who could not work from home (Angelucci et al., 2020[3]).

The following section details the extent to which different groups of workers could shift to remote work following the containment measures imposed by governments after the start of the pandemic. Distinguishing the capacity to work remotely across different groups is essential for identifying those with higher vulnerability during the crisis.

Box 3.1. Assessing the share of jobs amenable to remote working

There are two main methods for measuring the remote working potential of workers and firms. The first method measures the actual or potential rate through surveys conducted at the worker or firm level (Bloom ve et al., 2015; van der Lippe and Lippenyi, 2019; Hensvik et al., 2020; Adams-Prassl et al., 2020; Irlacher and Koch, 2020). Such surveys would include questions on the number of days of remote work practised by the workers, whether they could or would like to do it more, what factors limit their remote working practice or potential. Such surveys have the advantage of presenting precise information on the actual remote work practises adopted by the worker or the firms. On the other hand, small sample sizes in such surveys raise issues regarding representativeness or flexibility in the analysis due to statistical power. They also make international comparisons challenging.

The second method measures workers' capacity to work remotely by their occupation. It classifies each occupation based on the tasks required and according to the degree to which those tasks can be performed remotely (Dingel and Neiman (2020[4]), Saltiel (2020[5]) or Gottlieb, Grobovsek and Poschke (2020[6]). For example, occupations requiring workers to be outdoors (e.g., food delivery person) or to use heavy equipment (e.g., a vehicle) are considered to have a low potential of remote working. In contrast, occupations requiring only a laptop and an internet connection (e.g., an accountant, finance specialist, etc.) will have a high potential to work remotely. This method allows the use of the most recent administrative datasets that have broad coverage and allows international comparisons.

The analysis in this chapter classifies occupations based on a study by Dingel and Neiman (2020[4]) which is built from the O*NET surveys conducted in the U.S. As the occupations are classified according to the U.S. Standard Occupational Classification system (SOC), this note uses crosswalk to the International Standard Classification of Occupations (ISCO) to associate each occupation with a level of remote working potential in other countries (OECD, 2020[7]). Merging the occupation level information with labour force surveys makes it possible to assess the remote working potential of different groups (e..g, industries, income groups, etc.).

Sources: Adams-Prassl, A., Boneva, T., Golin, M., & Rauh, C. (2020). Inequality in the Impact of the Coronavirus Shock: New Survey Evidence for the UK.; Bloom, N., Liang, J., Roberts, J., & Ying, Z. J. (2015). Does working from home work? Evidence from a Chinese experiment. The Quarterly Journal of Economics, 130(1), 165-218; Hensvik, L., Le Barbanchon, T., & Rathelot, R. (2020). Which jobs are done from home? Evidence from the American Time Use Survey;. Irlacher, M; Koch, M. (2020). Working from Home, Wages,and Regional Inequality in the Light of COVID-19, CESifo Working Paper, No. 8232, Center for Economic Studies and ifo Institute (CESifo), Munich; van der Lippe, T., & Lippenyi, Z. (2020). Co-workers working from home and individual and team performance. New Technology, Work and Employment, 35(1), 60-79.

Remote working capacity varies significantly across industries and occupations

Remote working potential varies significantly across types of occupations. Due to the differences in the daily tasks, some jobs are more suitable for working from home. Figure 3.1 presents the share of workers who can work from home across the main occupation groups. For instance, amenability to remote working reaches 70% for managers and professionals, decreasing to less than 10% for elementary occupations, skilled agricultural, forestry and fishery workers, and craftspeople and related trades.

Figure 3.1. Remote working potential varies significantly across occupations

% of jobs amenable to remote working by occupation, 2019

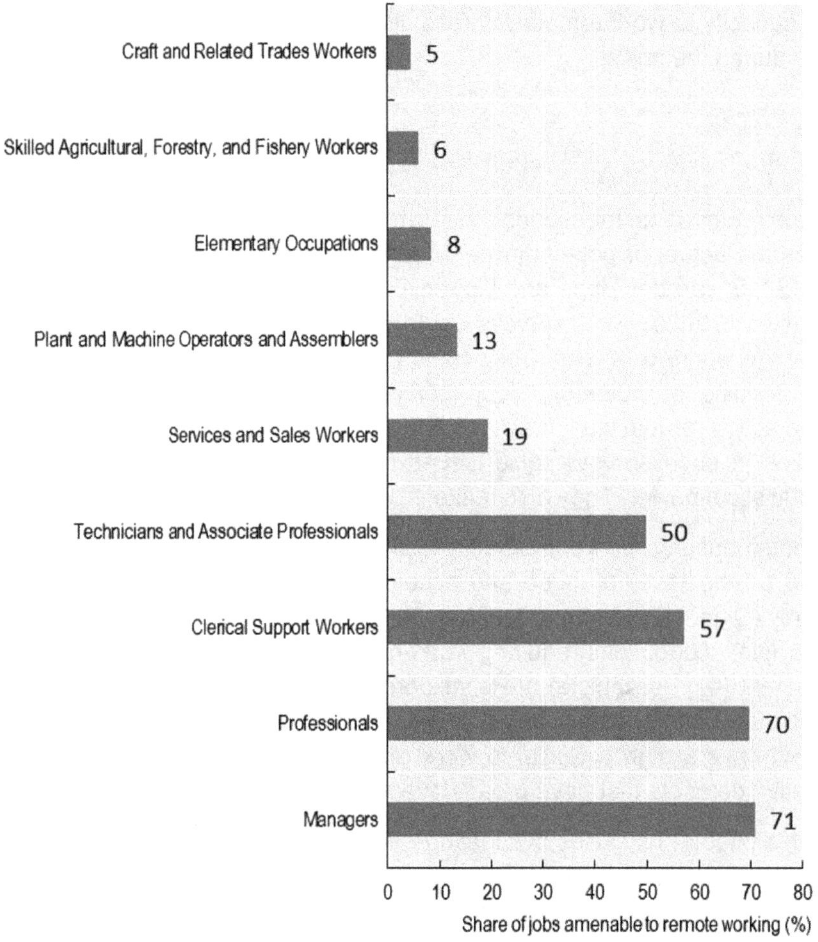

Note: The number of workers who can work remotely as the percentage of total workers in the occupation. Occupations are ranked in ascending order by the remote working potential in each occupation.
Source: OECD calculations based on European Labour Force Survey (2019), American Community Survey (2019), Canadian Labour Force Survey (2019) and Occupational Information Network data (accessed in March 2021).

StatLink https://doi.org/10.1787/888934248483

The share of jobs amenable to remote working also changes across industries. Industries' remote working potential depends on the occupational composition of their workers. For instance, while 75% of workers employed in the information and communication sector can work from home, this possibility decreases to 20% in construction, accommodation and food services activities, or agriculture. Overall, knowledge-intensive sectors that use digital tools have a higher potential to operate remotely, while those requiring physical effort or face-to-face interactions suffer larger disruptions.[1]

Figure 3.2. Some industries are more suitable than others to remote work

% of jobs that can be performed remotely by industry, 2019

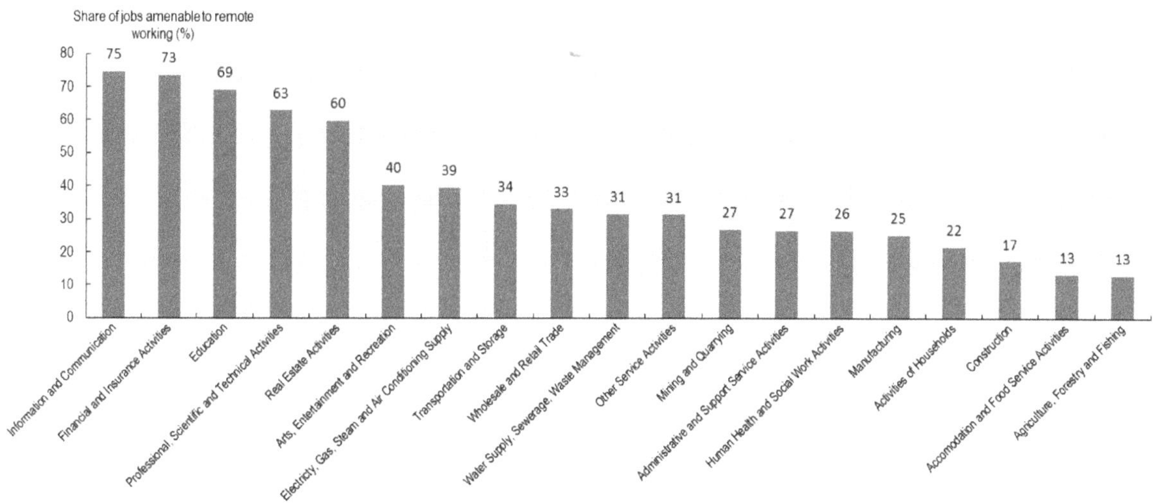

Note: The number of workers who can work remotely as the percentage of total workers in the industry. Industries are ranked in descending order by the remote working potential in each industry.
Source: OECD calculations based on European Labour Force Survey (2019), American Community Survey (2019), Canadian Labour Force Survey (2019) and Occupational Information Network data (accessed in March 2021).

StatLink https://doi.org/10.1787/888934248502

Education of the workforce and its remote working potential go hand in hand

The possibility of remote working correlates strongly with the skill requirement of the occupation. Workers with higher educational attainments are more likely to work in knowledge-intensive occupations not requiring a physical presence, which allows them to work remotely. Figure 3.2 illustrates the relationship between the share of workers with tertiary education (horizontal axis) and the share of workers who can work remotely (vertical axis) in the 2-digit ISCO occupation. The trend line shows that as the share of workers with tertiary education in the occupation increases, the share of jobs suitable to remote working also increases.

Differences in remote working potential across occupations are not only driven by skills. For example, science and engineering professionals or health professionals (e.g., doctors) are located below the trend line, indicating that the share of jobs amenable to remote working in these occupations is lower than expected, given the workforce's education levels. The technical equipment needs of science and engineering professionals, or the face-to-face interactions of health professionals, are important drivers of the observed differences after education is accounted for. On the other hand, managers or information and communications technicians are above the trend line and have higher rates of jobs amenable to remote working than expected from the workforce's skill composition.

Figure 3.3. Remote working potential increases with skill level in the occupation

% of jobs that can be performed remotely and workers with tertiary education, 2019

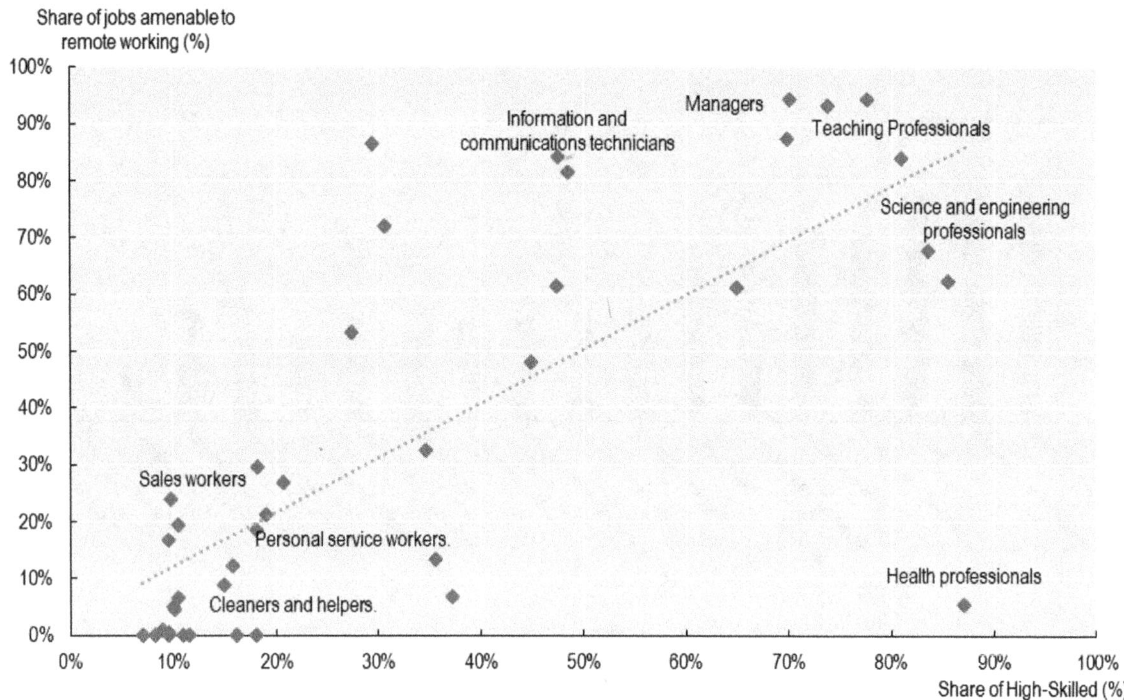

Note: The number of workers who can work remotely as a percentage of total workers in the occupation (vertical axis), and the share of workers with tertiary education in the same occupation (horizontal axis).
Source: OECD calculations based on European Labour Force Survey (2019), American Community Survey (2019), Canadian Labour Force Survey (2019) and Occupational Information Network data (accessed in March 2021).

StatLink https://doi.org/10.1787/888934248521

In Europe, the remote working potential is higher in more densely populated areas compared to other areas. Due to their industry structure and larger share of the high-skilled labour force, cities and dense urban areas are more likely to host occupations that can accommodate remote working. Indeed, using the "Degree of Urbanisation" (see Box 3.2 for more details) to distinguish different types of settlement for European countries, OECD evidence (2020[7]) demonstrates that cities (above 50 000 inhabitants) have a 13-percentage point higher share of jobs amenable to remote working than rural areas. Interestingly, the potential for remote working in towns and semi-dense areas seems to be somewhat closer to rural areas than to cities.

On average, cities and rural areas provide the highest and lowest remote working potential for workers of all skill groups. For example, while 58% of high-skilled workers can work remotely in cities, the share declines to 53% and 51% in towns and semi-dense areas or rural areas, respectively. Similar differences also exist for medium-skilled and low-skilled workers. The remote working gaps across regions are due to differences in the industrial structure, affecting occupational composition in the area.

Interestingly, the remote working potential gap between cities and rural areas is the smallest for high-skilled workers. For instance, the remote working potential of high-skilled workers in rural areas is 13% lower than those who work in cities. The gap is larger for low- and medium-skilled employees, at 26 and 30%, respectively. These differences suggest that the local economy's industrial structure affects the remote working potential of workers who are not high-skilled. On the other hand, the high-skilled workers are able to work remotely regardless of the industry that employs them.

Box 3.2. Defining skill groups

The analysis in this section classifies workers into three skill levels based on occupations (OECD, 2019):

- **Low skilled:** Jobs in sales and services and elementary occupations (ISCO 5 and 9)
- **Medium skilled:** Jobs such as clerks, craft workers, plant and machine operators and assemblers (ISCO 4, 7 and 8)
- **High skilled:** Jobs in managerial, professional, technical and associated professional occupations (ISCO 1, 2 and 3)

It is important to note this definition groups workers by their occupations' skill requirement and do not necessarily reflect the actual skill levels defined by workers' formal education. As shown in the literature, migrants often downgrade in the labour market, meaning that they work in occupations that are below their skill levels. This effect is possibly stronger for migrants arriving from non-EU countries as they face additional difficulties in degree recognition or residence permits.

Source: OECD (2019), Under Pressure: The Squeezed Middle Class, OECD Publishing, Paris, https://dx.doi.org/10.1787/689afed1-en.

Figure 3.4. Remote working is higher in cities for all skill groups

% of jobs that can be performed remotely by skill level and degree of urbanisation in European countries, 2019

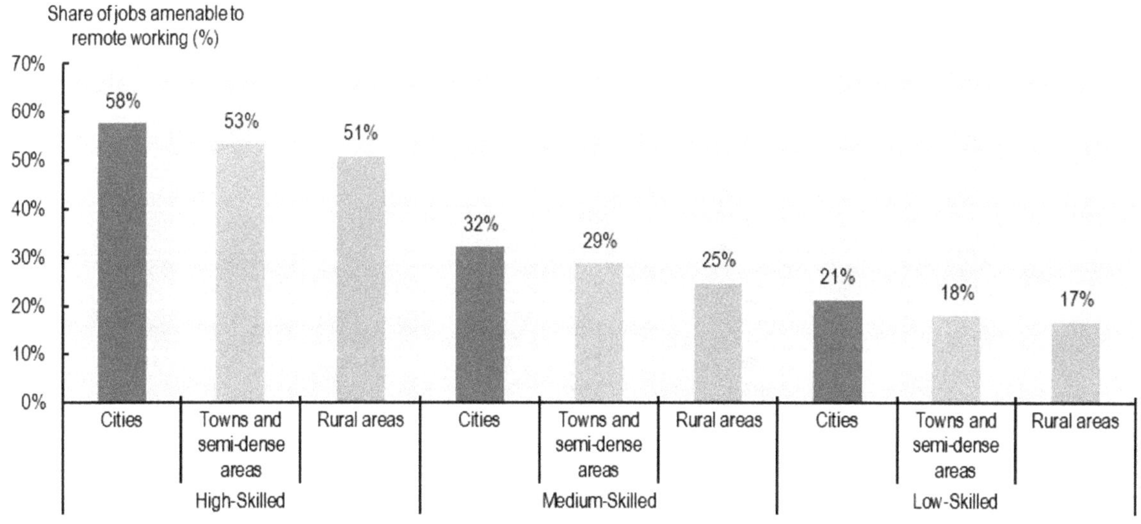

Note: The number of workers who can work remotely as a percentage of total workers in the skill group by the degree of urbanisation.
Source: OECD calculations based on European Labour Force Survey (2019), American Community Survey (2019), Canadian Labour Force Survey (2019) and Occupational Information Network data (accessed in March 2021).

StatLink https://doi.org/10.1787/888934248540

Remote working potential increases with wages

Remote working potential and wages are positively correlated. On average, occupations with higher remote working potential tend to have higher average wages. This is not surprising given that workers who can work remotely also tend to have higher education levels, as shown previously. Figure 3.5 presents the share of workers who can work remotely by income decile. Only one out of four workers who are in the first income decile (i.e., the 10% of workers earning the lowest salary) work in occupations that are amenable to remote working while this share increases to 61% in the 10th decile (i.e., the 10% of workers who are earning the highest salaries).

Box 3.3. The Degree of Urbanisation

The Degree of Urbanisation is a methodology to classify cities, towns and semi-dense areas, and rural areas for international comparison purposes. The method proposes three types of areas reflecting the urban-rural continuum instead of the traditional urban–rural dichotomy.

1. Cities: Densely populated areas with at least 50% of the population living in urban centres
2. Towns and semi-dense areas: Intermediate density areas where less than 50% of the population lives in rural areas and less than 50% of the population lives in urban centres
3. Rural areas: Thinly populated areas with more than 50% of the population living in rural areas

Source: Eurostat (2013), Urban-Rural Typology, http://ec.europa.eu/eurostat/web/rural-development/methodology, OECD (2020), OECD Regions and Cities at a Glance 2020, OECD Publishing, Paris, https://doi.org/10.1787/959d5ba0-en.

Figure 3.5. Better paid workers also have a higher remote working potential

% of jobs that can be performed remotely by wage decile, 2019

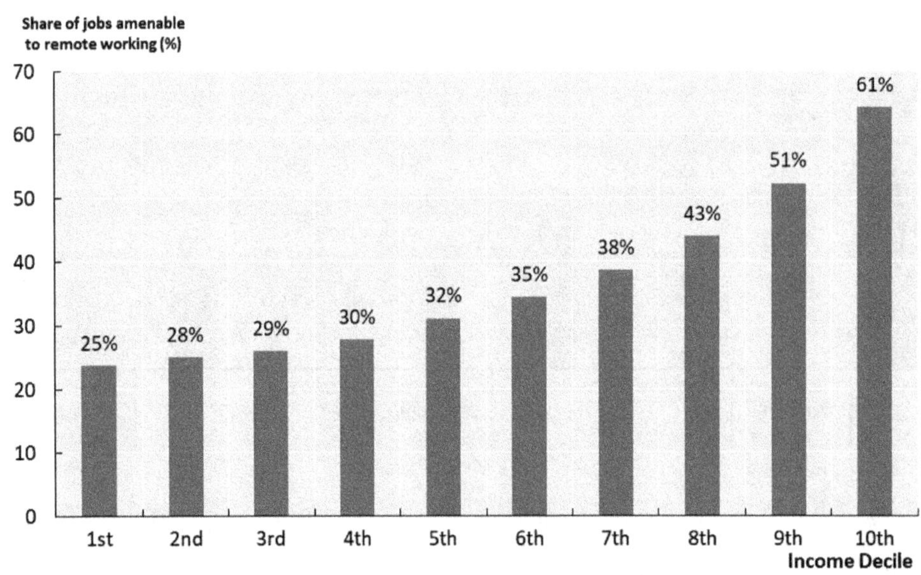

Note: The number of workers who can work remotely as a percentage of total workers in the income decile.
Source: OECD calculations based on European Labour Force Survey (2019), American Community Survey (2019), Canadian Labour Force Survey (2019) and Occupational Information Network data (accessed in March 2021).

StatLink https://doi.org/10.1787/888934248559

Unequal labour market effects of the pandemic: the case of the United States

The COVID-19 pandemic affected the United States labour market deeply, raising unemployment numbers and reducing labour force participation, wages, and hours worked. While the crisis has impacted the whole labour market, some workers have been affected more than others. To assess the impact of the pandemic on these labour market outcomes and explore its uneven effect across different types of workers, this section presents results from an econometric analysis for the United States. The analysis relies on data from the Current Population Survey (CPS), which includes more than 7 million individual records of workers over 2016-2021 and compares the evolution of labour market outcomes before and during the pandemic (see Box 3.4 for more details on the econometric analysis). First, the analysis compares the changes in workers' labour market outcomes with similar characteristics before and after the COVID shock and across different demographic groups. Second, it explores the differences in the outcomes between workers who were employed in occupations that are amenable to remote working and those who do not have jobs suitable to remote working.

The pandemic affected the U.S. labour market deeply

The pandemic affected all major labour market indicators in the U.S. Figure 3.6 presents the trend in labour market outcomes (vertical axis) over the period January 2018 to February 2021 (horizontal axis). The visuals show very large effects of COVID-19 on the U.S. labour markets, with a remarkable increase in the unemployment rate in March 2020 followed by a drastic increase in April 2020. More precisely, the unemployment rate increased from about 5% to 15% from February to April 2020. Following its peak in April 2020, the unemployment rate started declining gradually and dropped as low as 6% in December 2020.

The labour force participation also declined during the pandemic. Instead of entering unemployment, some workers dropped out of the labour force. More specifically, the participation rate decreased by 3 percentage points, from 62% to 59%, between March and April 2020, which corresponds to the largest monthly drop ever recorded in the U.S. (Lee, Park and Shin, 2021[8]). Interestingly, the sudden drop in the labour force participation rate turned out to be temporary. In fact, by July 2020, the participation rate had already bounced back to pre-crisis levels. However, since then, the participation rate has started its slow yet sustained decline, suggesting that some people who became unemployed might be discouraged to remain in the labour market. As these individuals exit the labour force, they reduce both the unemployment rate and labour force participation.

Since March 2020, the hours worked have slightly increased while the hourly wage has remained unchanged. One possible reason why hourly wages did not react to lower labour demand might be the slow adjustment of wages in the short run. Second, it is possible that workers with lower wages were the first ones to lose their jobs (Verdugo, 2016[9]). As these workers exit employment, the average wages of the remaining workers could have increased. If the wages dropped due to the lower labour demand during the crisis, the worker composition changes (i.e., where workers with lower salaries leave employment) and may have offset the decline as in the previous crisis. On the other hand, average working time per week increased by 1 hour, although it is difficult to understand whether it is due to the fact that workers who kept their jobs started working longer hours as in other recessions (Lazear, Shaw and Stanton, 2016[10]) or if those who worked in jobs requiring long hours of work managed to keep their jobs.

Figure 3.6. Covid-19 deeply affected the U.S. labour market

Hourly wage ($), hours worked per week, labour force participation rate (%) and unemployment rate (%)

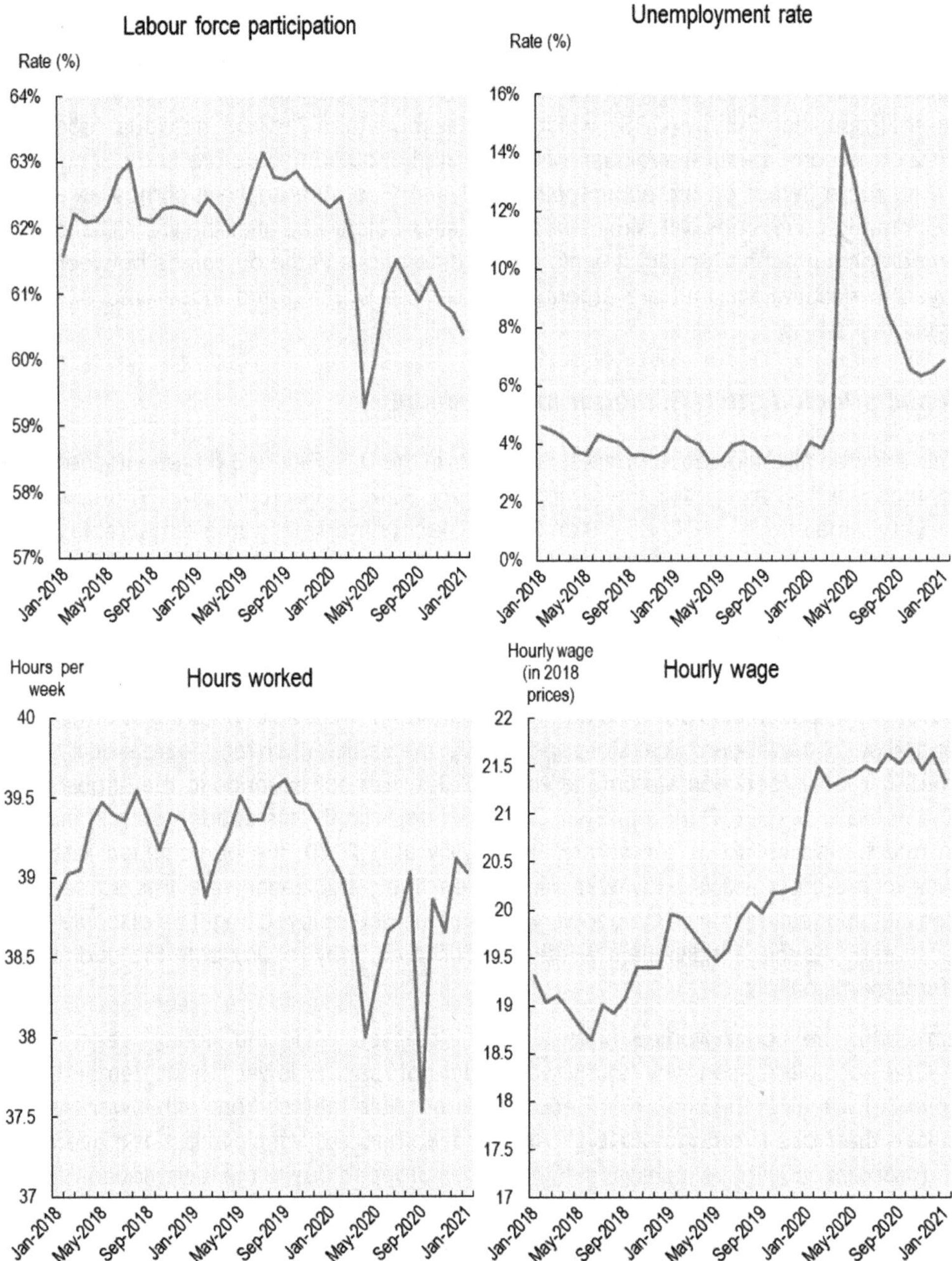

Note: The unemployment rate is calculated as the number of individuals who are unemployed as a percentage of the labour force. The labour force participation rate corresponds to the share of individuals at work, who held a job but were temporarily absent from work due to factors like vacation or illness, were seeking work, or were temporarily laid off from a job during the reference period as a percentage of the noninstitutionalised civilian population. The number of hours worked for civilians aged 16-70 who are employed and either at work or absent from work during the survey week, all jobs. Trimmed to exclude values below 1st percentile and above 99th percentile. Hourly wages cover civilians aged 16-70 currently employed as wage/salary workers, paid hourly, and were in outgoing rotation groups. Excludes self-employed persons. Trimmed to exclude values below the 1st percentile and above the 99th.

Source: OECD calculations based on the Current Population Survey (CPS).

StatLink https://doi.org/10.1787/888934248578

The short-run impact of COVID-19: An econometric analysis

Descriptive evidence presented in the previous section indicates that the COVID-19 crisis affected the labour market outcomes. While informative, these figures only provide suggestive evidence of the average effects across the labour market. However, early reporting on the labour market effects of the crisis suggests uneven consequences across different groups of workers. To address these questions, this section presents results from an econometric analysis as explained in Box 3.4

Using individual-level data, the regression analysis measures the change in individuals' labour market outcomes due to the COVID-19 pandemic. Figure 3.7 presents the regression results for the four labour market indicators, namely labour force participation rate, unemployment rate, average hours worked, and average hourly wages. Each panel presents results for a different labour market outcome, while each marker corresponds to the change since March 2020 (or Post-COVID) relative to the levels in the same month in the previous years for each population group. All the regressions take into account individual characteristics (such as education, age or sex) that may affect labour market outcomes. The analysis also accounts for the residence of the individual, as the crisis had an uneven effect across U.S. states. As such, the results should be seen as the change in the labour market outcomes for different groups, relative to the previous year and other groups that are also located within the same regional labour market.

The analysis shows that, since the beginning of the pandemic, there has been a substantial increase in the unemployment rate, a decrease in labour force participation, and a decrease in hours of work for all workers (Grey Marker) compared to the previous years. In contrast, no significant changes were observed for hourly wages. These effects, however, were uneven across groups. Young (aged 16 to 34), old (55 and above), low-skilled or migrant workers suffered the highest unemployment rate drops. While the unemployment rate increased by 3 percentage points for the overall population, the increase was larger, between 4-5 percentage points, for these most affected groups.

Similarly, these groups suffered the highest drops in labour force participation. As discussed above, while the hourly wages do not indicate any statistically significant change, the hours worked per week declined for all workers, more strongly for migrants and non-white minorities. Overall, these results suggest an increase in labour market inequalities.

Workers located in non-metropolitan areas were more than twice as likely to face unemployment compared to those located in metropolitan areas. The COVID-19 initiated discussions on whether the crisis would affect metropolitan areas more severely due to their higher reliance on the service sector, which requires face-to-face interactions (OECD, 2020[7]). Results from the econometric analysis (see Appendix) suggest that individuals located in non-metropolitan areas were more than twice as likely to be unemployed compared to those located in the same U.S. state yet in a metropolitan area.[2] On the other hand, the other labour market outcomes do not indicate any differential effect.

Figure 3.7. Unemployment increased, while labour force participation and hours worked declined

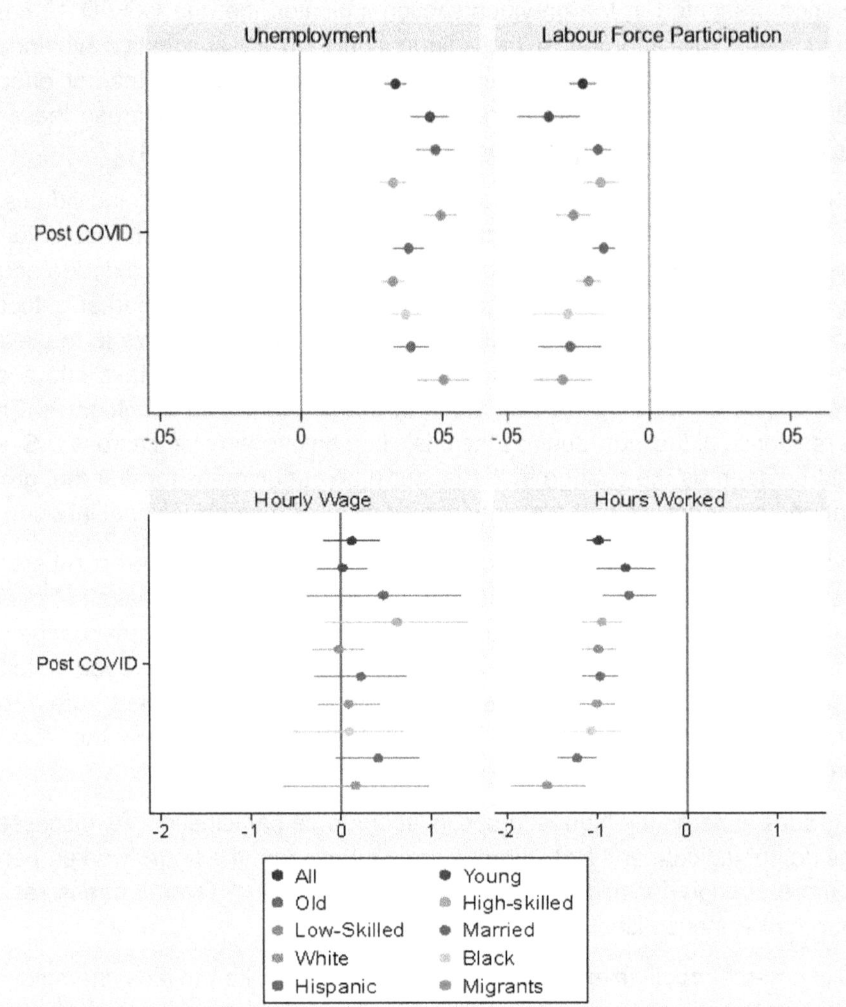

Note: Each panel presents regression results for a different labour market outcome. Each market corresponds to the coefficient (Post-COVID dummy) that captures the change in the labour market outcome since March 2020, relative to the levels in the previous years. Estimates are obtained from separate subgroup estimations. When possible, regressions control for individual characteristics (e.g., age, gender, education, marital status, race), state fixed-effects, month fixed-effects, year fixed-effects. Standard errors are clustered by U.S. states. The time period is January 2016 – January 2021.
Source: OECD calculations based on the Current Population Survey (CPS).

Box 3.4. Empirical strategy

The analysis in this section uses individual-level microdata and applies a simple pre/post strategy that has been used by other studies to study the effects of COVID-19 (Bacher-Hicks et al. 2020, Brodeur et al., 2021).

The estimation strategy relies on identifying the effects of the COVID-19 shock by comparing the evolution of labour market indicators for workers with similar observable characteristics (e.g., age, sex, education, etc.), before and after the COVID pandemic. The analysis uses the following model:

$$Y_{i,s,t} = \alpha + \beta PostCOVID_t + \gamma X'_{i,s,t} + \theta_s + \delta_t + \varepsilon_{i,s,t}$$

- $Y_{i,s,t}$ denotes the economic outcome for individual *i*, in state *s*, and month *t*. The four main outcome variables are *the unemployment rate*, *labour force participation*, *hours of work*, *hourly wages*
- $PostCOVID_t$ is an indicator equal to one for March and April 2020, and zero for all preceding months. The time period is January 2016 to January 2021
- $X'_{i,s,t}$ is a vector of demographic controls including age, gender, marital status and race
- θ_s is a state fixed-effect that absorbs structural differences between states
- δ_t is the time fixed-effect to account for cyclical differences by absorbing differences across months
- Standard errors clustered at the state-level

Data

The estimation is based on data from the Current Population Survey (CPS), collected by the Bureau of Labor Statistics (BLS), and provided by the Integrated Public Use Micro Samples (IPUMS). The CPS is a monthly survey of 60 000 eligible households. The CPS provides a large sample size of workers and individual characteristics such as age, education, race, and marital status and labour market characteristics such as labour force participation, employment status, hours of work, occupation and industry. The survey questions refer to activities during the week that includes the 12th of the month.

Source: U.S. Bureau of Labor Statistics: 2020, Frequently asked questions: The impact of the coronavirus (COVID-19) pandemic on The Employment Situation for March 2020. April 3, 2020. Bacher-Hicks, A, Goodman, J., Mulhern, C., 2021. "Inequality in household adaptation to schooling shocks: Covid-induced online learning engagement in real time" Journal of Public Economics, vol. 193. Brodeur, A., Clark, A.E., Fleche, S. and Powdthavee, N., 2021. "COVID-19, lockdowns and well-being: Evidence from Google Trends". Journal of Public Economics, vol. 193.

Remote working shielded workers against the adverse effect of the crisis

Prior to the COVID-19 pandemic, only a tiny share of workers made use of remote working opportunities. Remote working was considered an option that would provide workers flexibility, allowing them to work beyond office hours or to occasionally adjust their schedule depending on their family needs such as elderly or childcare. Prior to the COVID-19 pandemic, only one-fourth of workers using digital equipment at work had worked from home at least once a week in the E.U. (OECD, 2019[11]). In April 2020, close to 40% of workers in the E.U. were working from home on a full-time basis (Eurofound, 2020[12]). According to surveys, numerous companies worldwide consider shifting to mass teleworking permanently even after the COVID-19 health crisis will have abated (OECD, 2020[13]).

There are arguments based on economic theory suggesting that workers who could work from home during the pandemic face lower risks of job and income losses. Individuals who are able to keep their professional activities going are more likely to stay employed as they are able to produce and generate revenues for their enterprises. In other words, labour demand for occupations that can work remotely is likely to drop less severely than those which cannot. Evidence from jobs postings in European capitals indicates a consistent trend. While the number of job postings decreased dramatically across European capitals during the pandemic, the drop was more tempered for jobs with high remote working potential (Adrjan and Kleine-Rueschkamp, 2021[1]).

Despite the relevance of the issue, little is known about the importance of the remote working capacity for individuals' employment outcomes during the crisis. The remainder of this section explores the uneven effect of the crisis on workers who can work remotely versus those who cannot. First, it presents descriptive evidence on changes in the primary labour market indicators separately for both groups. In a second step, it presents more detailed evidence based on the econometric analysis.

Individuals with higher remote working potential were affected less severely

Before moving to the regression analysis, visualising the overall trends is important to get an initial idea about the differences in the labour market outcomes of workers who can and cannot work remotely. Figure 3.8 presents the evolution of labour market outcomes (vertical axis) over the period of January 2018 to February 2021 (horizontal axis) for workers by remote working potential. For the sake of simplicity, workers who are employed in occupations that have a remote working score above the mean are considered to be able to remotely work, while those below the mean are considered to be unable to work from home.

Before the crisis, labour market outcomes for both groups evolved similarly and labour market indicators exhibited different levels driven by the nature of occupations. On average, individuals working in jobs with high remote working potential participated more in the labour market, were less likely to experience unemployment, earned higher hourly wages and worked longer hours. Despite their differences, the visuals show that the two groups' labour market outcomes evolved in parallel trends until the crisis.

Labour market outcomes for both groups diverged during the crisis. The visuals show that the parallel change in both groups' trends was disrupted during the pandemic, and the outcomes started diverging. While both groups were affected by the crisis, workers with a below-average capacity of remote working were affected more severely. For example, while both groups experienced an increase in their unemployment rates by April 2020, the increase was significantly larger for those who cannot work from home. Similarly, a larger share of these workers dropped out of the labour force compared to workers who can work remotely.

Figure 3.8. Covid-19 triggered divergence in labour market outcomes between workers with high- and low-remote working potential

Hourly wage ($), hours worked per week, labour force participation rate (%) and unemployment rate (%), by remote working potential

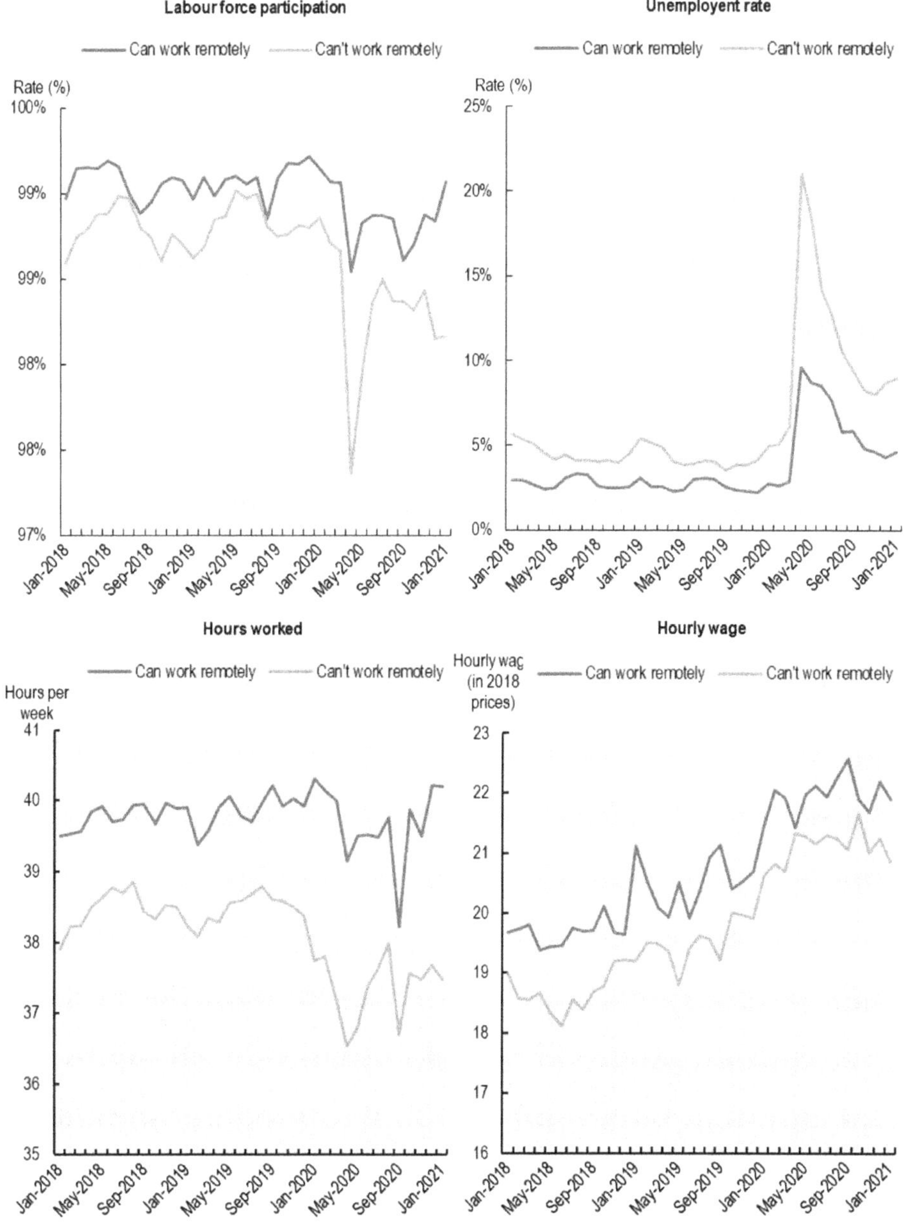

Note: Panels plot the evolution of labour market indicators separately for workers who can work remotely vs. those who cannot. Workers are categorised following the occupational classification of Dingel and Neiman (2020[4]). The unemployment rate is calculated as the number of individuals who are unemployed as a percentage of the labour force. The labour force participation rate is the share of individuals at work, held a job but were temporarily absent from work due to factors like vacation or illness; were seeking work, or were temporarily laid off from a job during the reference period as a percentage of the noninstitutionalised civilian population. The number of hours worked for civilians aged 16-70 who are employed and either at work or absent from work during the survey week, all jobs. Trimmed to exclude values below the 1st percentile and above the 99th percentile. Hourly wages cover civilians aged 16-70 currently employed as wage/salaried workers, paid hourly, and were in outgoing rotation groups. Excludes self-employed persons. Trimmed to exclude values below the 1st percentile and above the 99th.

Source: OECD calculations based on the Current Population Survey (CPS)

StatLink https://doi.org/10.1787/888934248597

The econometric analysis also confirms the divergence in labour market outcomes. Figure 3.9 presents the regression analysis for the four labour market indicators separately for workers with high and low remote working capacity. Each panel shows results for a different labour market outcome, while each marker corresponds to the change since March 2020 (or Post-COVID) relative to the levels in the same month in the previous years for each population group.[3] Results indicate that workers who cannot work remotely are twice as likely to be unemployed and 75% more likely to drop out of the labour force than those who can work. In contrast, there is no statistically significant difference in wages and hours worked.

Figure 3.9. Those who can work remotely were less affected by the crisis

Point estimates for labour market outcomes by remote working potential

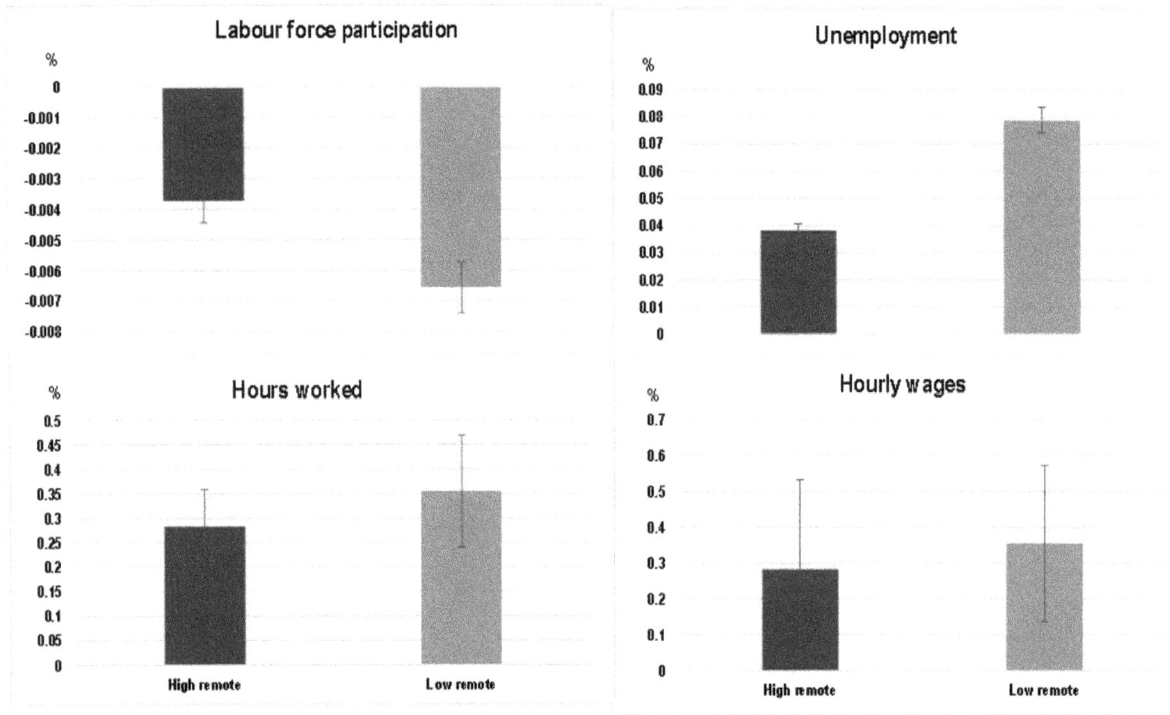

Note: Each panel presents regression results for a different labour market outcome separately for workers who can work remotely vs. those who cannot. Workers are categorised following the occupational classification of Dingel and Neiman (2020[2]). Each market corresponds to the coefficient (Post-COVID dummy) that captures the change in the labour market outcome since March 2020, relative to the levels in the previous years. Estimates are obtained from separate subgroup estimations. When possible, regressions control for individual characteristics (e.g., age, gender, education, marital status, race), state fixed-effects, month fixed-effects, year fixed-effects. Standard errors are clustered by U.S. states. The time period is January 2016 – January 2021.
Source:OECD calculations based on the Current Population Survey (CPS)

StatLink https://doi.org/10.1787/888934248616

Going beyond the pandemic: Rebuilding an inclusive labour market

The COVID-19 crisis has further exacerbated, in certain cases, pre-existing labour market inequalities. The labour market impact of the crisis has been highly uneven across workers. Similar to the previous crisis, once again, the most disadvantaged groups of workers, including low-skilled, low-wage workers, migrants and young people, have suffered the most in many OECD countries (Adams-Prassl et al., 2020[14]; Alstadsaeter et al., 2020[15]; Beland, Brodeur and Wright, 2020[16]; Belot et al., 2020[17]). Furthermore, these groups also lack the financial resources to deal with income losses, which make them vulnerable. As the workers who suffer from income losses also have little capacity to mitigate those shocks, income support can be an important rescue in the short run.

Young people have again been hit hard relative to the rest of the population, like during the global financial crisis (OECD, 2016[18]). This year's graduates, sometimes referred to as the "Class of Corona", are leaving schools and universities with often very poor chances of quickly finding employment or work experience. Meanwhile, their older peers are already experiencing the second heavy economic crisis in their still-young careers. The initial labour market experience profoundly influences the later working life, and a crisis can have long-lasting scarring effects on employment and earnings perspectives.

Job losses during the COVID-19 crisis will have effects that go beyond short-term income losses leading to negative long-term labour market outcomes. Individuals who experience employment losses during a large crisis suffer longer unemployment periods or must cope with lower-quality jobs (Davis and Von Wachter, 2011[19]). Many will find it hard to find a new job with similar responsibility, pay and career opportunity as the lost job. Workers who lose their jobs during a crisis, such as the current one, are also more likely to leave the labour market and become inactive. Looking at the Great Recession in the US, Yagan (2019[20]) shows that while unemployment rates recovered to their pre-crisis levels, the labour force participation rates declined and never recovered to their pre-crisis levels even six years after the end of the crisis. Thus, it is essential to develop active labour market policies that support workers who have lost their jobs during this period by encouraging their return to the labour market while helping them find good quality jobs.

Remote working will be part of the future

While containment measures have restricted economic activity in some sectors, the rapid expansion of remote working has helped maintain other jobs during the COVID-19 crisis. The disruptions to existing working arrangements caused by COVID-19 have led to a major increase in remote working out of necessity. Early in the crisis, Dingel and Neiman (2020[4]) suggested that some occupations might have greater remote working potential.[4] Evidence presented in the previous section suggests that workers with the capacity to work remotely are likely to have significantly lower risks of deterioration in labour market outcomes.

Remote working will be part of the future of work. However, predicting the actual share of remote workers once the health crisis will be over remains speculative. Remote working has many advantages for workers and firms, which indicates that there are reasons to believe that it will be part of the future. For instance, employees who work from home save time and money on commuting. Flexibility in working hours could also be preferable as it makes it possible to adjust working hours to the person's private needs, such as childcare. From the employer's perspective, such flexibility would reduce costs associated with renting or owning office space. Fewer people working on-site would allow firms to reduce rental costs, electricity and heating bills. In large cities such as London, New York or Tokyo, where office rents are high, office space reduction could substantially increase savings. In fact, surveys conducted across countries indicate that both employers and employees want to integrate remote working into their work-life even after the pandemic has receded (Taneja, Mizen and Bloom, 2021[21]).

Being able to work remotely will not benefit everyone equally, especially low-skilled workers. Individuals with a low level of formal education have little chance to work remotely due to the nature of their jobs' tasks. Such workers would not be able to seize such an opportunity, at least in the short run. While active labour market policies should be offered to help those who lost their jobs during the crisis back into employment, training programmes should be developed in parallel to upskill and prepare workers who are not able to work remotely.

Conclusion

The COVID-19 pandemic has led to a health crisis and to a labour market shock, putting unprecedented pressure on people, places, and firms. While people were forced to stay home under lockdowns, economic activity was interrupted, leading to declining GDP and rising unemployment. In many countries, the adverse labour market effects were particularly strong for already disadvantaged groups of workers, often overrepresented outside dense cities.

Relying on in-depth analysis on the U.S., the chapter also shows that workers living outside metropolitan areas were twice as likely to face unemployment as workers living in metropolitan areas. Without measures to support the large portions of workers hard hit by the pandemic, the current crisis stands to worsen further the conditions of already vulnerable groups and areas, potentially exacerbating already stark regional inequalities.

Remote working will be part of the future. As remote working becomes a permanent component of professional life, it will present new opportunities and bring about certain changes. As shown in Chapter 2, remote working has a strong regional dimension, with significantly higher concentrations of occupations amenable to remote working in dense regions or regions with easier access to cities. This chapter looks at how remote working could potentially influence the future through the lens of several individual characteristics, which are likely causing the observed spatial gaps, notably between cities and many areas with a lower population density. These characteristics include education, skills, and labour market outcomes. For example, highly skilled people are more likely to have jobs that are compatible with remote working, but rural areas offer lower remote working potential across all types of skills compared to cities.

How governments address the new normality of remote working will affect both territorial inequalities and those based on socio-economic conditions. It is essential that policies encourage the return to the labour market jointly address the unemployment crisis and the transition to remote working while simultaneously taking into consideration the socio-economic characteristics of the labour force within territories.

References

Adams-Prassl, A. et al. (2020), "Inequality in the Impact ofthe Coronavirus Shock: Evidence from Real Time Surveys", *CEPR Discussion Paper* 14665. [14]

Adrjan, P. and L. Kleine-Rueschkamp (2021), *After the Boom? COVID-19 and European City Labour Market*, HiringLab, https://www.hiringlab.org/uk/blog/2021/02/19/after-the-boom-covid-19-and-european-city-labour-markets/. [1]

Alipour, J., H. Fadinger and J. Schymik (2021), "My home is my castle – The benefits of working from home during a pandemic crisis", *Journal of Public Economics*, Vol. 196, p. 104373, http://dx.doi.org/10.1016/j.jpubeco.2021.104373. [2]

Alstadsaeter, A. et al. (2020), "The First Weeks of the Coronavirus Crisis: Who Got Hit, When and Why? Evidence from Norway", *NBER Working Paper* 2131. [15]

Angelucci, M. et al. (2020), "Remote Work and the Heterogeneous Impact of COVID-19 on Employment and Health", *National Bureau of Economic Research*, http://dx.doi.org/10.3386/w27749. [3]

Beland, L., A. Brodeur and T. Wright (2020), "COVID-19, Stay-at-Home Orders and Employment: Evidence from CPS Data", *IZA Discussion Paper* 13282. [16]

Belot, M. et al. (2020), "Unequal Consequences of COVID-19 across Age and Income: Representative Evidence from Six Countries", *IZA Working paper* 13366. [17]

Bick, A., A. Blandin and K. Mertens (2020), "Work from Home After the COVID-19 Outbreak", *Federal Reserve Bank of Dallas, Working Papers*, Vol. 2020/2017, http://dx.doi.org/10.24149/wp2017r1. [22]

Davis, S. and T. Von Wachter (2011), "Recessions and the cost of job loss". [19]

Dingel, J. and B. Neiman (2020), "How Many Jobs Can be Done at Home?", *Becker Friedman Institute White Paper* March, https://bfi.uchicago.edu/working-paper/how-many-jobs-can-be-done-at-home/. [4]

Eurofound (2020), *Living, working and COVID-19: First findings – April 2020*, https://www.eurofound.europa.eu/publications/report/2020/living-working-and-covid-19-firstfindings-%0Aapril-2020. [12]

Gottlieb, C., J. Grobovsek and M. Poschke (2020), "Working from home across countries", *COVID economics*, Vol. 8. [6]

Lazear, E., K. Shaw and C. Stanton (2016), "Making Do with Less: Working Harder during Recessions", *Journal of Labor Economics*, Vol. 34/2. [10]

Lee, S., M. Park and Y. Shin (2021), "Hit Harder, Recover Slower? Unequal Employment Effects of the Covid-19 Shock", http://dx.doi.org/10.3386/W28354. [8]

OECD (2020), "Capacity for remote working can affect shutdowns' costs differently across places", *OECD COVID-19 Policy Note*, http://www.oecd.org/coronavirus/policy-responses/capacity-for-remote-working-can-affect-lockdown-costs-differently-across-places-0e85740e/. [7]

OECD (2020), “Exploring policy options on teleworking: Steering local economic and employment development in the time of remote work”, *OECD Local Economic and Employment Development (LEED) Papers*, Vol. 2020/10. [13]

OECD (2019), *Measuring the Digital Transformation: A Roadmap for the Future*, OECD Publishing, Paris, https://dx.doi.org/10.1787/9789264311992-en. [11]

OECD (2016), *Society at a Glance 2016: OECD Social Indicators*, OECD Publishing, Paris. [18]

Saltiel, F. (2020), “Home working in developing countries”, *COVID economics*, Vol. 6. [5]

Scarpetta, S., A. Sonnet and T. Manfredi (2010), “Rising youth unemployment during the crisis: How to prevent negative long-term consequences on a generation?”, *OECD Social, Employment and Migration Working Papers, No. 106*, Vol. 106/106, pp. 1-47, http://thefamilywatch.org/doc/doc-0077-es.pdf. [23]

Taneja, S., P. Mizen and N. Bloom (2021), “Working from home: The polarising workplace”, *Vox EU blogpiece*, https://voxeu.org/article/working-home-revolutionising-uk-labour-market. [21]

Verdugo, G. (2016), “Real wage cyclicality in the Eurozone before and during the Great Recession: Evidence from micro data”, *European Economic Review*, Vol. 82, pp. 46-69, http://dx.doi.org/10.1016/j.euroecorev.2015.11.001. [9]

Yagan, D. (2019), “Is the Great Recession Really Over? Longitudinal Evidence of Enduring Employment Impacts”, *Journal of Political Economy (Forthcoming).* [20]

Notes

[1] Remote working is viable only assuming the continuation of the activity in the sector as a whole. However, if demand in a specific sector collapses completely, all workers employed in the sector will suffer and may have to cease working, regardless of whether their occupation could be performed remotely or not (OECD, 2020[7]).

[2] Individuals are grouped into metropolitan and non-metropolitan areas based on the variable METRO provided in the CPS data, which refers to the household location.

[3] Like in the previous analysis, all the regressions take into account individual characteristics (such as education, age or sex) that may affect the labour market outcomes, and the residence of the individual as the crisis had uneven affect across states. As such, the results should be seen as the change in the labour market outcomes for both groups, relative to the previous years and to one another within the same local labour market.

[4] Data on actual remote working in the US during the crisis confirmed that Dingel and Neiman's occupational classification captured well the remote working potential (Bick, Blandin and Mertens, 2020[22]).

Annex 3.A. Technical Appendix

Definitions of variables

- *The unemployment rate*: The number of persons unemployed as a percentage of the total labour force.
- *Labor force participation*: Individuals in the labour force who are currently employed; held a job but were temporarily absent from work due to factors like vacation or illness; were seeking work; or were temporarily laid off from a job during the reference period.
- *Hours of work*: Computed for civilians aged 16-70 who are employed and either at work or absent from work during the survey week, including all types of jobs. Hours of work is trimmed to exclude values below the 1st percentile and above the 99th percentile.
- *Hourly wages*: The hourly wages (in 2018 constant dollars) is computed for civilians aged 16-70 currently employed as wage/salary workers, paid hourly and were in outgoing rotation groups. It excludes self-employed persons, and we trim to exclude values below the 1st percentile and above the 99th percentile.

Descriptive statistics

Annex Table 3.A.1. Descriptive Statistics

	No. of observations	Mean	S.D	Max	Min
Labour force participation	5 229 284	0.62	0.48	0	1
Unemployed	3 195 149	004	0.21	0	1
Real hourly wages (2018 dollars)	352 931	19.1	10.35	9.08	101.73
Hours worked last week	2 695 661	39.13	12.12	1	100

Note: The labour force participation rate corresponds to the share of individuals currently employed, held a job but were temporarily absent from work due to factors like vacation or illness; were seeking work, or were temporarily laid off from a job during the reference period as a percentag of the noninstitutionalised civilian population. Number of hours worked for civilians aged 16-70 who are employed and either at work or absent from work during the survey week, all jobs. Trimmed to exclude values below the 1st percentile and above the 99th percentile. Hourly wages covers civilians aged 16-70 currently employed as wage/salary workers, paid hourly, and were in outgoing rotation groups. Excludes self-employed persons. Trimmed to exclude values below the 1st percentile and above the 99th.
Source: OECD calculations based on the Current Population Survey (CPS)

StatLink https://doi.org/10.1787/888934248635

Regression results

Annex Table 3.A.2. The impact of COVID-19 on labour market outcomes by different worker groups

	Unemployment	Labour Force Participation	Hourly wage	Hours worked
All	0.0569 (0.003)***	-0.0194 (0.002)***	0.1178 (0.154)	-0.9856 (0.066)***
Young	0.0858 (0.006)***	-0.0350 (0.005)***	0.0133 (0.136)	-0.6834 (0.163)***
Old	0.0540 (0.004)***	-0.0119 (0.004)***	0.4709 (0.421)	-0.6435 (0.144)***
High-Skilled	0.0370 (0.003)***	-0.0163 (0.003)***	0.6195 (0.393)	-0.9495 (0.108)***
Low-Skilled	0.0697 (0.004)***	-0.0208 (0.003)***	-0.0284 (0.139)	-0.9888 (0.090)***
Married	0.0448 (0.003)***	-0.0156 (0.002)***	0.2122 (0.256)	-0.9687 (0.100)***
White	0.0532 (0.003)***	-0.0174 (0.002)***	0.0800 (0.173)	-1.0062 (0.095)***
Black	0.0688 (0.005)***	-0.0270 (0.006)***	0.0846 (0.306)	-1.0710 (0.164)***
Hispanic	0.0766 (0.006)***	-0.0252 (0.006)***	0.4020 (0.233)*	-1.2262 (0.108)***
Migrants	0.0769 (0.007)***	-0.0283 (0.007)***	0.1551 (0.405)	-1.5544 (0.205)***
Observations	3 653 951	6 003 971	399 658	3 024 769
Individual characteristics	Yes	Yes	Yes	Yes
State Fixed-Effect	Yes	Yes	Yes	Yes
Month Fixed-Effect	Yes	Yes	Yes	Yes
Year Fixed-Effect	Yes	Yes	Yes	Yes

Note: Each column presents regression results for a different labour market outcome, while each row corresponds to the estimates for each worker group. The coefficients correspond to the Post-COVID dummy that has captured the change in the labour market outcome since March 2020, relative to the levels in the previous years. Estimates are obtained from separate subgroup estimations. When possible, regressions control for individual characteristics (e.g., age, gender, education, marital status, race), state fixed-effects, month fixed-effects, year fixed-effects. Standard errors are clustered by U.S. states. The time period is January 2016 – January 2021. The number of observations refers to the regressions with the entire sample.
Source: OECD calculations based on the Current Population Survey (CPS)

StatLink https://doi.org/10.1787/888934248654

Annex Figure 3.A.1. Labour market outcomes for metropolitan and non-metro areas

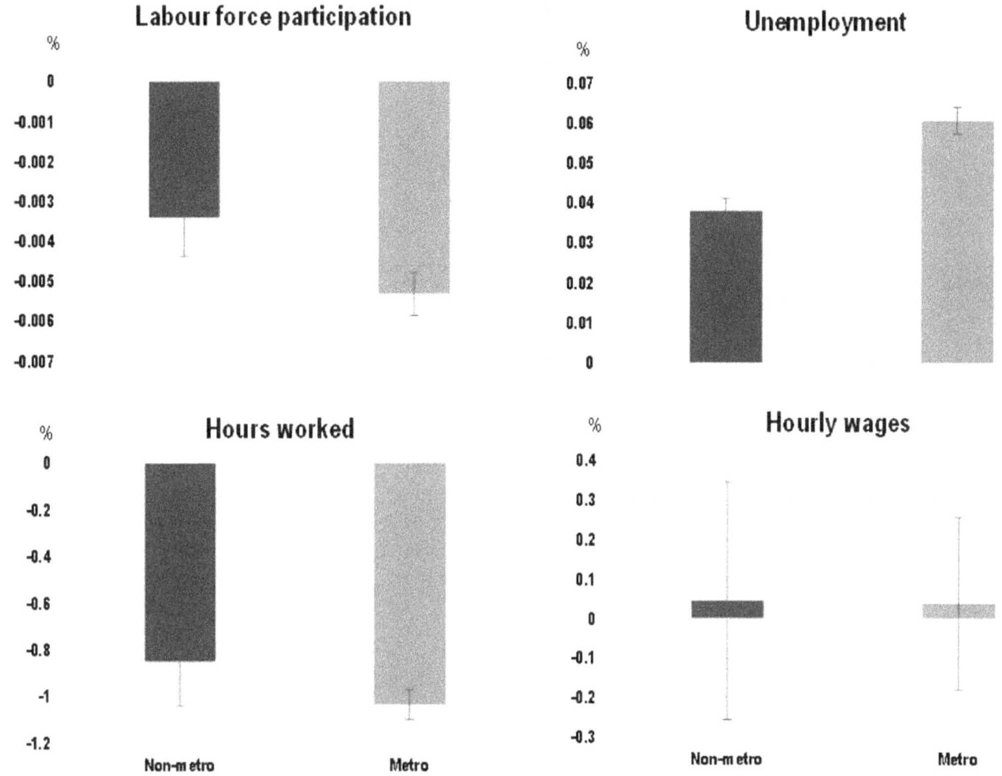

Note:Each panel presents regression results for a different labour market outcome separately for workers located in metropolitan areas vs. those who do not live in a metropolitan area. Each market corresponds to the coefficient (Post-COVID dummy) that has captured the change in the labour market outcome since March 2020, relative to the levels in the previous years. Estimates are obtained from separate subgroup estimations. When possible, regressions control for individual characteristics (e.g., age, gender, education, marital status, race), state fixed-effects, month fixed-effects, year fixed-effects. Standard errors are clustered by U.S. states. The time period is January 2016 – January 2021.
Source:OECD calculations based on the Current Population Survey (CPS)

Annex Table 3.A.3. The impact of COVID-19 on labour market outcomes by different remote working potential

	Unemployment	Labour Force Participation	Hourly wage	Hours worked
High remote work	0.0383 (0.003)***	-0.0037 (0.001)***	0.2834 (0.249)	-1.0128 (0.076)***
Low remote work	0.0788 (0.005)***	-0.0066 (0.001)***	0.3551 (0.218)	-1.0534 (0.114)***
Observations	3 346 375	3 363 894	376 941	2 791 579
Individual characteristics	Yes	Yes	Yes	Yes
State Fixed-Effect	Yes	Yes	Yes	Yes
Month Fixed-Effect	Yes	Yes	Yes	Yes
Year Fixed-Effect	Yes	Yes	Yes	Yes

Note: Each column presents regression results for a different labour market outcome separately for workers who can work remotely vs. those who cannot. Workers are categorised following the occupational classification of Dingel and Neiman (2020[2]). Each market corresponds to the coefficient (Post-COVID dummy) that has captured the change in the labour market outcome since March 2020, relative to the levels in the previous years. Estimates are obtained from separate subgroup estimations. When possible, regressions control for individual characteristics (e.g., age, gender, education, marital status, race), state fixed-effects, month fixed-effects, year fixed-effects. Standard errors are clustered by U.S. states. The time period is January 2016 – January 2021.
Source: OECD calculations based on the Current Population Survey (CPS)

StatLink https://doi.org/10.1787/888934248673

4 Post-COVID-19 spatial effects and policy responses for G7 countries

This chapter sets out possible effects of COVID-19 on the adoption of remote working models and spatial distribution of people and firms, and outlines existent and needed G7 policy responses to benefit from these new trends. The chapter begins by reviewing the results from recent research and surveys on the effects of COVID-19 on remote working adoption and on the spatial decisions of workers and firms. Then, it outlines the G7 policy strategies at national and regional levels to make the most of remote working and attract people and firms. Finally, the chapter examines the policies needed to enhance the long-term attractiveness of non-metropolitan regions.

Introduction

The Covid-19 crisis has brought manifold changes to the way people interact and firms do business, but with unequal effects across the territory. The COVID-19 crisis has accelerated the trend of digitalisation, allowing a higher share of workers to continue their economic activity from home and many firms to function virtually, without a common physical workplace. Yet, as previous chapters have depicted, the capacity to adopt remote working methods is unequal among type of regions, workers and firms. Notably, large cities are the places with the greatest share of the labour force that is capable of working remotely because of the larger share of well-paid and high educated workers in high-value added service activities. Looking at the post-pandemic scenario, governments need to put in place forward –looking policies to help all regions seize the benefits of remote working and prepare for changes in settlement patterns.

This digitalisation of economic interactions has opened the possibility for workers and firms to reassess where to live and locate, which can reduce the attractiveness of cities, although a massive exodus from cities is unlikely. Cities have historically attracted most workers and firms due to benefits from **physical** agglomeration of economic actors. Greater acceptance and adoption of **virtual** working methods and social interactions offer new incentives for workers and firms to relocate outside high densely populated areas. These incentives include access to affordable and bigger housing and office spaces and to environmental amenities. Yet, densely populated areas will likely retain most workers and firms, as they benefit from economies of agglomeration and will also seek ways to transform and improve quality of life.

Irrespective of the post-pandemic scenario and the decision of workers and firms to relocate across the territory, policies need to be forward looking and responsive if they are to seize the potential benefits that remote working and other technologies can offer. Emerging technologies coupled with a greater adoption of remote working will continue to disrupt the benefits of physical proximity and the way people and firms interact, which could lead to new forms of mobility for a share of the population. Policies have then a decisive role in the future attractiveness of regions and the environmental and economic outcomes in the new normality.

This chapter sets out possible effects of COVID-19 on the adoption of remote working and the spatial distribution of people and firms, and outlines current and required policy responses to benefit from these new trends. The chapter begins by reviewing the results from recent research and surveys on the effects of COVID-19 on remote working adoption and on the spatial decisions of workers and firms. Then, it outlines the G7 policy strategies at national and regional levels to make the most of remote working and attract people and firms. Finally, the chapter examines the policies needed to enhance the long-term attractiveness of non-metropolitan regions.

COVID-19's effects on remote working and on the spatial distribution of people and firms

The COVID-19 pandemic has accelerated the adoption and acceptability of remote working. As Chapter 2 and 3 depicted, during the COVID-19 crisis many firms and workers have embraced remote working as a common practice and relied on it even during the months it was not compulsory. The increasing adoption of remote working coupled with a greater digitalisation of services and human interactions might offset some of the central forces behind economic agglomeration in cities. This section revises recent academic literature and official and private surveys on the long-term effect of COVID-19 on remote working adoption and on the spatial distribution of people and firms.

Working remotely will likely persist but under a hybrid model

COVID-19 has led to an unprecedented growth of teleworking. This crisis led many firms to accommodate their business models to function remotely and workers to change labour habits by working at home. Although prior to the COVID-19 outbreak, teleworking used to be treated chiefly as a matter of opportunity to improve employee's work-life balance, during the pandemic it became a mainstream standard in many professional environments. Remote working is a new experience for many, and it has proven to have a number of benefits and challenges for people and firms.

Benefits and challenges of remote working

Working at home has proven to bring benefits for people and firms in a number of economic, social and environmental areas:

- **Economic benefits**:
  - **For firms**: remote working enlarges the pool of workers that firms can choose from (e.g. high skilled workers who, for personal reasons, are tied to a specific location), which can decrease labour costs and improve skill-matching. Furthermore, with a share of employees working at home, firms could reduce some costs on office space, utilities or services. Remote working can also improve and normalise co-operation among satellite offices within the same company and open new business opportunities to meet teleworkers' needs.
  - **For workers:** remote working reduces commuting expenses and creates labour opportunities for women, people with disabilities or the elderly (Chapter 2). It also offers the flexibility to have multiple jobs and to relocate to reduce housing and living costs.
  - **For society**: Remote working can spread wealth across the territory by allowing mobility – temporary or permanently – to different locations.
- **Social and environmental benefits:**
  - **For workers**: This labour practice can improve work-life balance by allowing workers to spend more time at home with the family and decreasing commuting time.
  - **For society**: Remote working can have an impact on the reduction of global greenhouse emissions, air pollution and transport congestion, resulting in lower levels of air pollution.

However, remote working also revealed a number of shortcomings in economic, social and environmental areas. As explained in Chapter 2 and 3, the unequal capacity to adopt remote working based on the type of region, type of worker or type of firm is a chief challenge for the future. However, some of the challenges in adopting remote working might include the speed and the compulsory nature of this labour practice coupled with lockdowns and the technology available until now.

- **Economic challenges**:
  - **For firms**: a greater adoption of teleworking raises questions around innovation and team cohesion. It also creates challenges for team management and limits the gains from information and knowledge spill overs inside and among firms. The cost associated with adopting digital technologies and management reorganisation is a sizeable challenge, particularly for small firms.
  - **For workers**: Disparities in access to telework add to existing dimensions of income inequality. Well-paid workers and those in high value-added service activities are often more likely to telework, while those with lower incomes and performing in-person services do not have the same possibilities. It adds to the cost of utilities and equipment at home. Career progression and networking is also perceived as a shortcoming of teleworking, especially for young people.
- **Social and environmental challenges**:

- **For firms**: Corporate culture belonging to a company might be affected by employee retention and engagement.
- **For workers**: Inappropriate working environment at home, high levels of multitasking with children, isolation, hidden overtime and blurry boundaries between private and work life, with consequences on health (OECD, 2020[1]). Many workers found themselves working at home with children and in unsuitable spaces and work conditions, especially young and low-income workers (Gorlick, 2020[2]). Moreover, the Covid-19-related economic crisis has exacerbated inequalities among type of workers, based on education, economic activity and gender (Chapter 2 and 3).
- **For society**: remote working might lead to a change in the mobility patterns of workers and greater individual consumption of resources at home (e.g. water, energy) which would require a readjustment of the strategy to attain climate goals due to lower gains from efficiencies of agglomerations (e.g. waste management, building energy efficiency).

Figure 4.2 summarises main challenges and benefits of teleworking during the recent scenario of short-term adaptation to this new working practice.

Figure 4.1. Advantages and disadvantages of teleworking for businesses and people

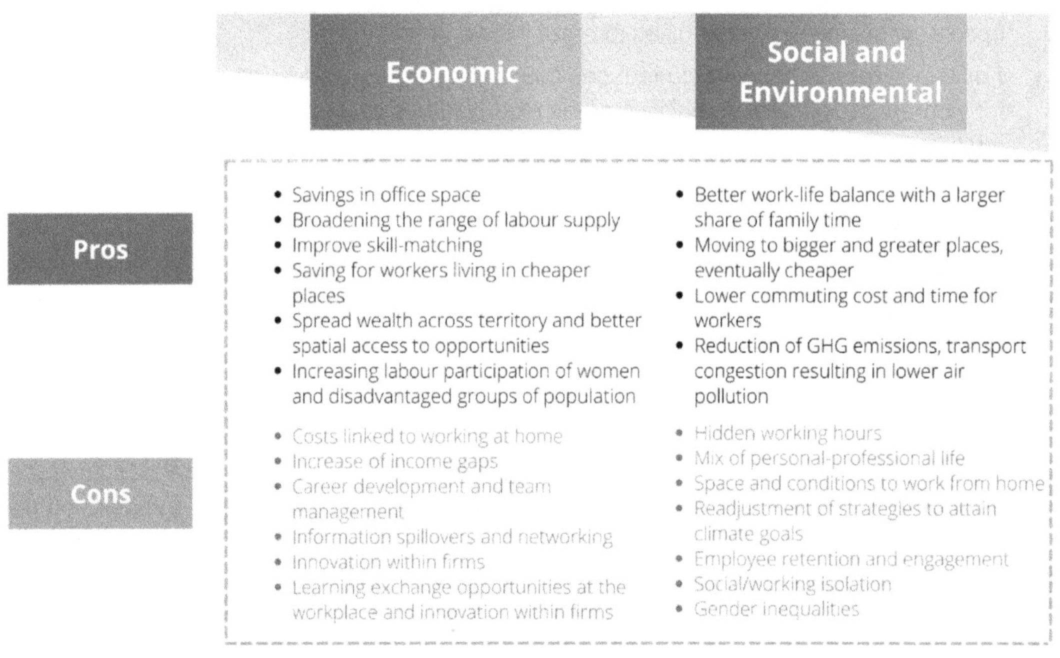

Source: OECD own elaboration.

Net impact of remote working on productivity remains uncertain with signs for optimism

Although the net effects on productivity levels are not yet clear, the results seem to be better than expected. Prior to the pandemic, the literature on productivity of working from home was relatively scarce. According to studies in the US and China before COVID-19, workers experienced an 8% to 13% increase in productivity due to working from home (Emanuel and Harrington, 2020[3]; Bloom, 2015[4]).[1] During the pandemic, the net effect of remote working on productivity remains unclear, as other factors affected workers' performance and well-being, such as lockdowns, mobility restrictions and the speed of the transition.

On the positive side, several studies, mainly through self-reported assessments, highlight the positive effect of telework on productivity during the pandemic:

- According to (Barrero, Bloom and Davis, 2020[5]), out of a sample of 1 500 workers in the US, 84.7% reported a similar or higher level of productivity from being at home than in the office. These authors estimate that productivity levels with remote working could increase by at least 2.4%, taking into account that this scenario involves other effects affecting productivity (e.g. children at home, pandemic-related stress) (Barrero, Bloom and Davis, 2020[5]).
- During May and June 2020, the Boston Consulting Group surveyed 12 000 employees in *teleworkable* activities in United States, Germany and India, of whom 75% reported being at least as productive in performing their individual tasks as they were before the pandemic (BCG, 2020[6]).
- In May 2020, a survey by YouGov, LinkedIn and USA Today covering 2 001 US adults showed that 54% of respondents stated that remote working had a positive effect on their productivity (YouGov, USA TODAY & LinkedIn, 2020[7]).
- Etheridge et al. (2020[8]), using self-reported survey data from the UK, found productivity at home is not significantly different from productivity in the workplace.

However, the conditions under which remote working unfolded makes it difficult to disentangle the net effect on productivity. A firm-survey in Japan underlined that employers perceived a lower productivity level of workers who adopted remote working during the pandemic (40% less than at the workplace on average), yet the effect varies across industries - information and telecommunications industry had the highest productivity, while retail the lowest (Morikawa, 2020[9]). The reported factors affecting productivity include outdated regulations for some tasks, poor telecommunications environment at home, and psychological effects of the health crisis, among others.

Companies have only just begun to apply the best available techniques for remote working. As technology is quickly advancing (e.g. use of virtual reality for meetings) and regulations are being revised, productivity benefits from remote working can be a target for industries and governments to improve in the future.

The increasing acceptability of hybrid remote working

Some surveys and authors have pointed to a post-pandemic scenario where a hybrid model of working is preferred by workers and firms. Hybrid remote working refers to a combination of time between working at home and at the workplace that varies from reduced working time at home, flexible approaches or only occasional presence at the workplace (Figure 4.2). A number of recent surveys reveal increased intentions from both managers and workers to keep remote working practices in place after the pandemic fades (Table 4.11). Nevertheless, some other surveys raise uncertainties about the extent of teleworking (Indeed, 2021[10]) .

Figure 4.2. Hybrid telework spectrum

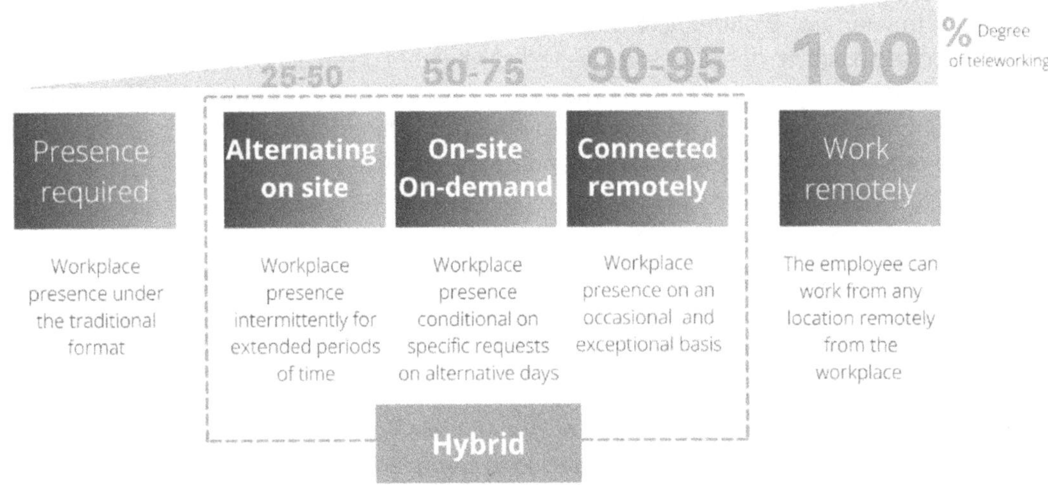

Source: Own elaboration based on (BCG, 2020[6])

A common characteristic of the surveys analysed is the positive perception on the outcome of remote working and expectations that this working model will continue to a greater extent than before the pandemic (Table 4.1). For example, a survey of 500 managers in Germany shows that a large majority of them (89%) agree that the home office can be implemented on a larger scale without disadvantages, while a global survey from PWC (133 business and 1 200 office workers) reveals that a greater share of employers (83%) agree that remote work has been successful in their companies, in comparison with pre- pandemic scenarios. Specifically in most of the surveys, a hybrid teleworking model is the most likely working system to be implemented in the medium term (e.g. France 58% of respondents and in the United States 62%), in countries like Italy the concept of smart working (remote working but without fixed working hours) reported positive outcomes on productivity.

However, many respondents to these surveys agree that some strategies still need to be put in place to improve teleworking conditions. A survey in France (2 049 employees) highlights an important share of employees (40%) have felt isolated during the remote working periods, which can be explained by lockdown measures. Surveys in countries such as Italy and Germany highlight the relevance of adaptation of a regulatory framework for teleworking, the training of managers and supervisors with remote teams or career progression. The aggregate effect of the share of remote working time and the number of workers adopting this labour practices is still uncertain.

Table 4.1. Selected surveys on effects and perception of remote working during the pandemic, a focus on G7 countries (2020 and 2021)

Scope	Source/Institution	Year	Sample	Survey results
France	(Harris Interactive, 2020[11])	November 2020	2 049 people	• 70% teleworked at least partially and 45% teleworked full time; 30% were exclusively face-to-face. • 39% of employed people say that their current job cannot be carried out by teleworking, compared to 36% who say they can telework without difficulty. • 58% of employees believe in a hybrid model • 40% of employees who had teleworked during the week of the survey felt isolated

Canada	(Statistics Canada, 2020[12])	May 2020	Not specified	• 22.5% of businesses expect that 10% or more of their workforce will continue to telework or work remotely • 25% of Canadian business are 'likely' or 'very likely' to offer their employees the option to work remotely following the pandemic, while 14% will make it a requirement
Germany	(IAO, 2020[13])	May 2020	500 managers	• 70% of the companies, employees work entirely or mainly in their home office. 21% a hybrid model. • 58% of the companies had no home office regulation or company agreement becoming the main obstacle to telework • 89% agree with the statement that the home office can be implemented on a larger scale without disadvantages. • 75% of respondents also believe that their employees will in the future ask to work from home more often
	(IAB-Forum, 2020[14])	December 2020	1 723 establishments	• 43% of all employees receiving welfare benefits and marginal employment (14.1 million people) had the opportunity to work from home in May this year • 50% worked more than 20 hours per week from home in May 2020 compared to 8% of the previous year
Italy	(McKinsey & Company, 2020[15])	April 2020	5 000 service workers	• 64% of respondents rate their managers as either sufficiently or poorly prepared to manage their team. • 83% of respondents intend to continue to work from home • In general, respondents are convinced that smart working (remote working but without fixed working hours) has increased efficiency
	(Corriere della Sera, 2020[16])	June 2020	4 000 public employees	• 88% judge the experience (transition to telework) as successful and 93% would like to continue. • 34.3% say they have increased their working hours thanks to smart working • 68.3% did not receive specific training in teleworking • For 30% of public servants it was not possible to get a room to work and for 11% was difficult to work while family members were doing other things (e.g. watching TV, attending virtual school classes, cooking)
United States	(Ozimek, 2020[17])	April 2020	1 500 hiring managers	• 61.9% of hiring managers interviewed in a recent US poll stated their intention to rely more on remote work in the future • The expected growth rate of full-time remote work over the next five years has doubled, from 30% to 65%
United Kingdom	(Indeed, 2021[10])	March 2021	Not specified	• 60% of remote jobs posted by employers were marked as 'temporarily remote' during Lockdown 3 in early 2021 • 40% of remote postings of jobs are described as non-temporarily remote
	(Office for National Statistics UK, 2020[18])	July 2020	18 000 households	• 46.6% of employed people did some work at home • 34.4% worked fewer hours than usual and 30.3% more hours • 57.2% of people living in London did some work at home, though this less likely for people aged 16 to 24 years of age
Global	(PWC, 2021[19])	June 2020	133 executives and 1 200 office workers	• 83% of employers say the shift to remote work has been successful in their companies, compared to 73% in June 2002 • 55% of employees want to work remotely three days a week or more
	(BCG, 2020[20])	June 2020	12 000 employees	• 40% of their employees will follow a remote-working model in the future • 37% of companies expect that more than 25% of employees will work in hybrid models that combine remote and onsite work

Digitalisation and working from home might improve the attractiveness of low density populated areas

The long-term response of people and firms as a consequence of increased teleworking practices might lead to the relocation of some economic actors outside of densely populated cities, although a mass exodus from cities seems unlikely. Some workers with greater abilities to remote work might be attracted to move outside cities to less densely-populated places that offer housing that is cheaper and bigger with better environmental amenities. Some large firms, mainly technological companies have already given their employees the possibility to work from home permanently (e.g. Twitter or Shopify). Yet, the exodus from populated places is not likely as economies of agglomeration would keep attracting business and workers based on greater network opportunities, entertainment and cultural amenities.

Cities have historically been the most attractive places for firms and workers…

Cities have spearheaded economic success and living standards within countries, while attracting people at a rapid pace. The population living in cities, high-density places of at least 50 000 inhabitants, has more than doubled over the last 40 years (OECD/European Commission, 2020[21]). The agglomeration economies of cities have historically attracted capital, firms, consumers and workers whose physical proximity creates a number of benefits, including a better match of supply and demand for labour, greater offer of goods and entertainment activities. Density of cities has also a positive effect on exchange of ideas, innovation and productivity. OECD estimates point toward a productivity gain of 2-5% for a doubling of population size (OECD/European Commission, 2020[21]).

The attractiveness of cities is not only economic, as city residents also benefit from higher standards of living. Urbanisation and development are closely interlinked (Glaeser and Gottlieb, 2009[22]). Agglomeration increases the efficiency of health and education provision and offers citizens greater access to cultural amenities and social life. Educational attainment is considerably higher in cities than in rural areas, due to a greater concentration of universities and technological centres.

… But increasing adoption of remote working can reduce the appeal of cities

As cities keep growing in size, agglomeration effects also create a number of shortcomings. Cities tend to face higher prices of land and housing and a reduced offer of environmental amenities. Urban residents are more exposed to crime, health related issues, violence and air pollution than residents elsewhere (OECD/European Commission, 2020[21]). For many workers, especially in cites with poorly developed public transport, commuting to work takes an important share of the daily time and represents a high cost. It is also a source of stress and safety concerns.

The appeal of cities is dwindling

The arrival of COVID-19 and lockdown measures tarnished some of the attraction of cities, while it exacerbated some of their shortcomings. In many countries, lockdowns were coupled with restrictions on in-person services and cultural amenities such as restaurants, bars or theatres. With the greater adoption of remote working, many people found themselves in small and unsuitable conditions for working at home, while paying relatively high housing (rent, utilities, maintenance) and living costs (e.g. food and utility prices). In fact, a share of urban residents, mainly high earning workers or students with family elsewhere, moved temporarily outside cities, breaking the trend of the last decades of inflow population to the cities (see Chapter 1).

Central business districts in large cities have experienced most of the outmigration during COVID-19. In the largest US cities, this effect was greater among people living in high-income neighbourhoods (Ramani and Bloom, 2021[23]; Liu and Y Su, 2020[24]). People in these neighbourhoods (e.g. Manhattan) have greater incentive to relocate as they are most likely able to work remotely and own secondary houses, while paying high rents and housing prices. Also, during the lockdown periods, the in-person entertainment amenities (restaurants and bars) were shut down, which make it much less attractive to live in those neighbourhoods. For example, during lockdown periods of 2020, Tokyo experienced the first net outmigration since 2013 (Ministry of Land, Infrastructure, Transport and Tourism of Japan, 2020[25]).

Some effects of the temporary outmigration have led to a moderate decrease or stagnation of prices in housing and office space in cities. In many local markets, firms are increasingly reluctant to rent or buy new space while waiting for changes in remote working, which has driven forecasting scenarios of price stagnation in the next couple of years (Credit Suisse, 2020[26]). In 2020, the annual growth of housing prices in capital cities like London (3.5% 2020 vs 2019) or Paris (5.4% for apartment prices 2020 vs 2019) grew below the national average (8.5%, 6.3% respectively) (UK HPI, 2021[27]) (Notaires-Insee, 2021[28]).

Ramani and Bloom (2021[23]) estimated that the top 10% zip codes with highest population density in the central business districts of the 12 largest metropolitan areas in the US experienced more than a 10% drop in rents, while the rent prices in areas with lower population density remain stable or slightly increased. Similarly, the effect on residential and commercial property prices in the 12 largest metropolitan areas in the US decreased relatively more than in less densed populated areas.

While the appeal of places with low population density increasing

With a greater possibility and acceptability of remote working, the arguments in favour of leaving big cities are certainly greater than before the pandemic. The lower living costs and increased affordability of larger spaces in more rural regions are particularly relevant for people. Some people could also value the possibility to be closer to nature and enjoy outdoors activities, while others can see it as an opportunity to leave stress of cities and change their way of living. For businesses, the possibility to relocate outside a city or downscale their offices or headquarters is under much debate. While surveys so far are inconclusive, a common threat is an increasing number of companies expecting to modify their real estate decisions.

The analysis of recent surveys in G7 countries reflects a greater willingness of people to move outside cities and firms' expectations to modify building offices in cities, in comparison to pre-COVID scenarios.

- A study in the UK showed that 15% of people surveyed were considering moving out of the city as a result of life in lockdown. Almost one-third (34%) stated they think differently about their home as result of the COVID-19 outbreak, especially the importance of a garden and the need for more indoor space for homeworking (Nationwide, 2020[48]).
- A survey in Japan conducted by the national government showed that 46% of respondents said they were more interested in moving outside the capital city. Moreover, 14% of the companies surveyed have started to consider offshoring or relocating their headquarters out of Tokyo (for more information, see the (Box 4.1).
- The AEI Housing Centre has found that between May and August 2020, buyers have opted for homes in areas with 19% less density on average than the same period last year. Demand was up 74% in the least dense quintile of zip codes (Tobias and Pinto, 2020[29])).
- A survey in Italy found that 85% of people surveyed "would go or return to live in the South if they were allowed to, and if it were possible to keep their jobs remotely". These are young people with a university degree, professional experience and, in 63% of cases, with a permanent contract (Lanari, 2020[30]). Moreover, COVID-19 has also driven requests for properties in the countryside. Thanks to the lockdown period and the massive use of smart working, the demand for farmhouses outside the big cities has soared by 30% compared to the same period in the pre-COVID era (Immobiliare, 2020[31]).
- A survey in the US showed that a majority (87%) of executives expect to make changes to their real estate strategy in the medium-term. These plans include consolidating not only office space in prime locations but also opening more satellite locations (PWC, 2021[32]).

Box 4.1. Results from a survey in Japan

In April 2020, Japan's government (like numerous other governments) announced a state of emergency due to COVID-19 infections and gave governors greater legal authority to urge people to stay indoors and businesses to close. Unlike in many Western countries, enforcement relies more on peer pressure and Japan's deep-rooted tradition of respect for authority, rather than imposing fines.

The Ministry of Land, Infrastructure, Transport and Tourism conducted a series of surveys in the summer of 2020 to find out more about the effects of telework on the location decisions of companies and employees after COVID-19. The first survey was addressed to 375 companies that have their headquarters in Tokyo. It aimed to find out about companies' plans for teleworking after COVID-19. Some 53% of respondents said telework will continue, while 18% said it will increase. The survey also sought to find out companies' plans for offshoring as a result of COVID-19. Based on this feedback, 26% of the companies surveyed are considering offshoring or relocating their headquarters. Some of these companies had considered this even before the pandemic (12%), whilst others started to consider it with the onset of Covid-19 (14%).

Figure 4.3 Headquarters' relocation plans from enterprises based in Tokyo

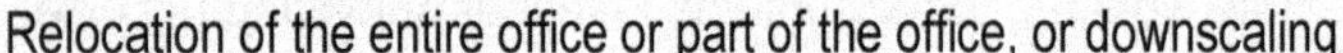

Relocation of the entire office or part of the office, or downscaling

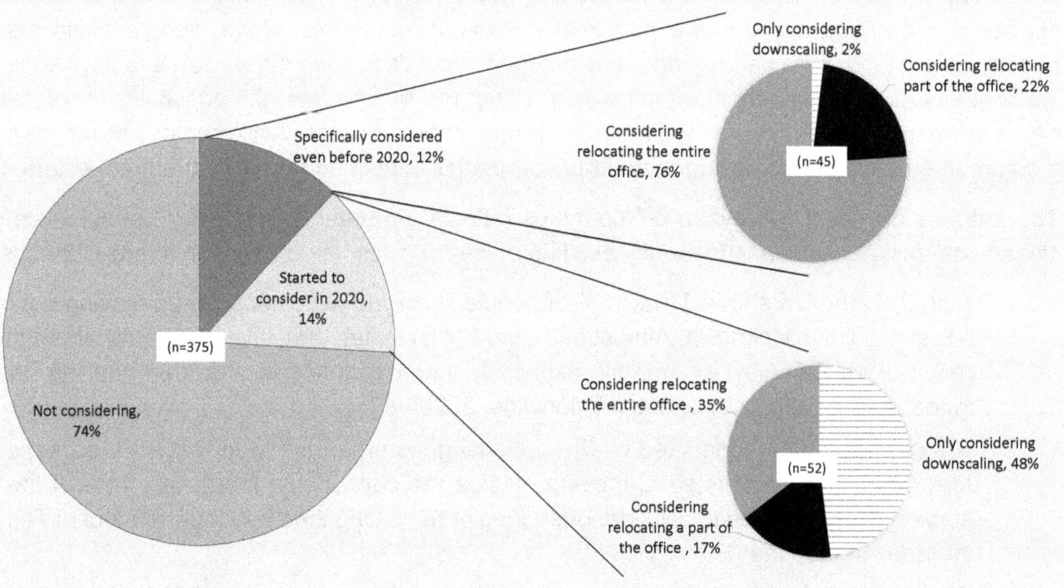

Note: The figure on the left depicts responses from 375 enterprises headquartered in Tokyo regarding the willingness to relocate a specific department/division or the entire headquarters. The figures on the right highlight the type of change in headquarters' strategies from the enterprises considering relocating out of Tokyo.
Source: MLIT (2020[33]), Questionnaire on remote working conducted to enterprises headquartered in Tokyo (August 2020)

The second survey, conducted among 1,078 people over 20 years old in Tokyo, asked about the intention of workers in Tokyo to move to rural areas after COVID-19 and the ideal working style. The results show that 46% of people surveyed were slightly or significantly more interested in moving to rural areas than previous the pandemic. When asking about the ideal working method, most workers said they would choose a hybrid model of living part of the time in a rural area and the rest of the time in an urban one.

Figure 4.4. Workers' interest in working location after COVID-19

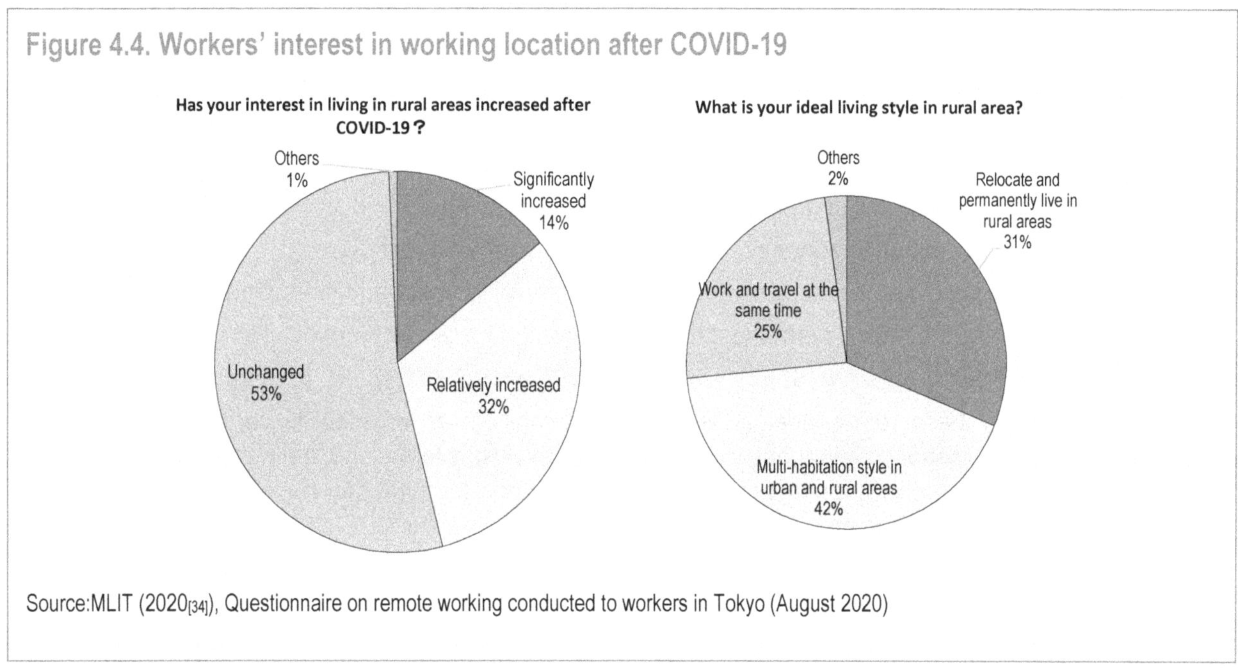

Source:MLIT (2020[34]), Questionnaire on remote working conducted to workers in Tokyo (August 2020)

Yet, a permanent outmigration from cities is unlikely and undesirable.

Despite the greater adoption of remote working, benefits from agglomeration economies will likely be a predominant factor to retain workers and firms in cities. As mentioned before, physical proximity in densely populated areas creates efficiency on economic, social and environmental factors. Exchange of ideas, innovation and business creation are factors that are highly dependent on face-to-face contact and these interactions are a source of productivity, growth and increased well-being. The relevance of in-person social interaction for people also leads to a demand for leisure and cultural amenities, (e.g. bars, restaurants and theatres) which tend to benefit from proximity to highly populated areas. Furthermore, efficiency of economies of scale facilitate a more sustainable management of resources and the attainment of climate goals. These agglomeration benefits will be harder to replace with virtual interaction in the short term.

In fact, in the scenario of greater migration away from cities, the dispersion of settlements could bring negative effects on various fronts, including the environment, income of low-skilled workers in large cities or efficiency of service delivery.

- Efforts to achieve the climate agenda could be undermined by potential sprawl as remote working becomes increasingly popular. The degree of urbanisation creates economies of scales that are relevant to reduce negative effects on the environment. These places also concentrate higher efficiencies regarding resources management (e.g. wastewater reuse, IT infrastructure), transport (e.g. public transport, commuting) and public service delivery (e.g. gas, water) (Newman and Kenworthy, 2000[35]).
- An increasing use of a hybrid work model could also reduce aggregate income of lower-skilled workers in cities. As mentioned before, high-skilled workers in cities are the share of the workforce with the greatest capacity to telework. Low-skilled service workers in large cities, who are heavily dependent on jobs requiring physical presence, bore the brunt of the economic impact of the recent pandemic (Althoff et al., 2020[36]). An intermittent presence of these types of workers in central business districts could affect income of local consumer service industries that rely heavily on their demand.
- Efficiency of service provision could also be affected as cities benefit from scale to provide high quality services, education and health, with an easier access to them.

Four scenarios of the distribution of settlement pattern in the post-COVID-19 world

Despite the uncertainties at the time of elaborating this report, with the pandemic still unfolding, four possible future settlement pattern scenarios could emerge in the new normality as workers and firms increasingly embrace remote working. They include:

1. business as usual but with greater adoption of remote working
2. expansion of commuting zones around cities as a doughnut effect, with
3. a rise of intermediate cities in terms of attractiveness for workers and firms, and
4. structural changes from a permanent movement of high-skilled workers outside city centres (name it "City Paradox").

Table 4.2 describes these four scenarios and their possible effects on mobility patterns and regional development. These scenarios might not occur in mutually exclusive forms and the linkages between them may vary in time (some can happen before others) and space (regions can have different scenarios). Figure 4.5 ilustrates these four scenarios.

Table 4.2. Scenarios of the distribution of settlement patterns in the post-COVID-19 world.

	Description	Degree of workers' relocalisation and changes in firm's real estate strategies	Effect on mobility and regional development
Business as usual with greater use of hybrid working model	Dense cities continue to agglomerate workers and firms. Remote working is increasingly adopted within the city, with little impact on the workers' relocation.	Low: Most workers remain in large cities by favouring proximity to workplaces. -Some firms with teleworkable activities still limit possibilities of remote working.	-Reduce pressure on public transport at peak times in large cities and increased use during off-peak times. -Increased one-off commuting to telework outside cities, either in secondary houses or rented spaces. -Non-metropolitan regions with tourist attractions have greater inflows throughout the year.
Doughnut effect	The city centre becomes more hollow or empty, as businesses and people move to the outskirts of the city to find affordable and larger housing.	Medium-Low: High-skilled workers move from large cities to their outskirts or areas with bigger and cheaper spaces. - Workplaces in the CBD become friendly/attractive spaces that promote social interactions.	-Increase distance of commuting, but per person commuting time reduces. -Outskirts and rural regions face new demand for services and land. -Improve housing affordability within large cities. -Greater demand for expansion of public transport services in some large cities.
The rise of intermediate cities	Cities offering agglomerations and medium services benefit from the drain of densely populated cities. Workers and firms seek the advantages of these cities' balanced quality of life.	Medium-High: Workers with highly teleworkable activities move to intermediate cities. -Firms reduce headquarters and open satellite offices. -Increase co-working spaces in intermediate cities	- Greater demand for services and land in intermediate cities. - House and office prices stagnate or reduce in large cities, relative to other cities. - Increase use of car in intermediate cities with poorly developed public transport.
City paradox	Highly skilled workers move outside central business districts. It reduces income for workers (mostly low-skilled) in local consumer service industries in cities, which might trigger movement of these workers outside the city.	High: An important share of high-skilled and low-skilled workers leave large cities and spread out across the territory. -Increase in nomad workers (mainly young) with a greater use of hotels and touristic areas as workplaces. -Increase in co-working spaces across the territory	-Long but less frequent commutes by nomad workers (car, train and plane). - Decreased general commuting time, but more short commutes by car. -Rise of co-working centres in non-metropolitan regions/ outskirts of the city. -Small cities and rural regions face greater demand for services and land. -CBD struggler and are reconverted into housing districts or green areas.

Note: These four scenarios are built based on relevant articles available at the moment of this publication. The Doughnut effect scenario is inspired by (Ramani and Bloom, 2021[23]). The rise of intermediate cities scenario is inspired by a work in progress by Philipp McCann; the City Paradox is based on (Althoff et al., 2020[36]), while the Business as usual with more remote working world was built from internal discussions at the OECD. CBD refers to Central Business Districts.

Figure 4.5. Scenarios of the distribution of settlement patterns in the post-COVID-19 world (graphic description)

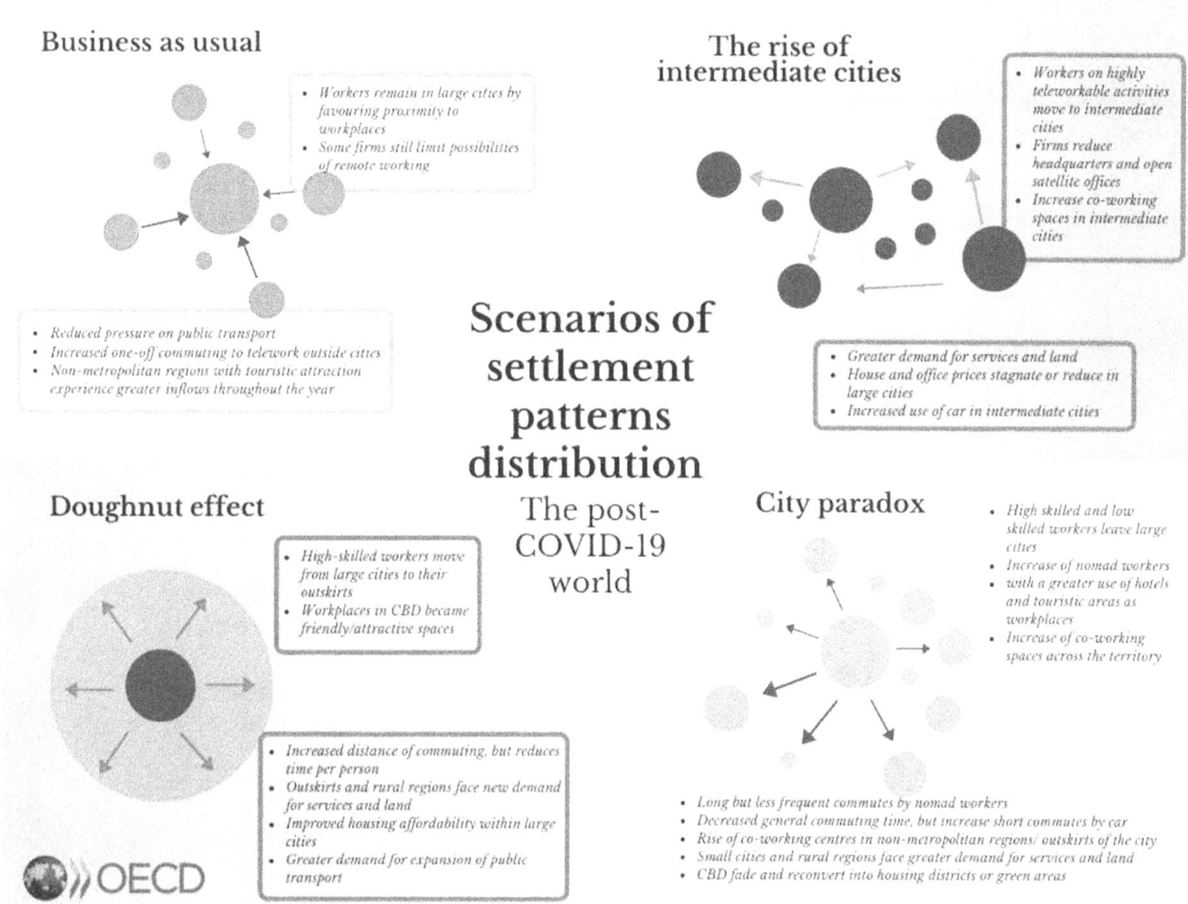

Note: CBD refers to Central Business Districts

Whether the post-pandemic world is closer to one of those scenarios, to a combination of some or to none, one thing is likely: the greater acceptance of virtual working methods and social interactions. Any greater magnitude of remote working adoption could imply greater consumption of resources at home and new commuting patterns for some workers. In some cities, a relocation of workers would lead to new demand for transport connections or longer distances commuted by car.

Furthermore, remote working is only one of several practices and technologies that can modify location and mobility patterns in the future (Box 4.2). In the long run, the cumulative effect of this new labour model with technologies such as virtual or augmented reality or automotive vehicles can modify the incentives for workers and firms to live or locate to different places than current ones (OECD, 2020[37]). Technological progress might also allow in-person activities such as hairdressers or sales to conduct services virtually (or through robots). While the future has many uncertainties, technology will certainly keep disrupting the way people interact and the benefits from physical proximity.

Governments should thus establish flexible policies to adapt to changes in settlement patterns, especially with land use and public transport policies as well as the promotion of resources efficiency and circular economy practices among households. The long-term preparedness of local governments and co-ordination policies to improve structural attractiveness and factors for development (including energy efficiency) of all regions is of chief importance for benefiting for any future scenario.

Box 4.2. Technologies impacting rural economies and communities

Technology is changing rapidly. Every year, new and improved types of devices and services become available on the market. Many of these technologies have the potential to improve rural economies, their production processes and the traditional economic sectors. New technologies also modify how people access public services and interact with society.

OECD (2020[37]) mapped a number of technologies that will shape the future of rural regions. While many technologies are undergoing rapid transformation and promise disruptive effects, the identified technologies could potentially change rural communities in particular.

Table 4.3. Key technologies driving rural change

Technologies		Opportunities for rural regions	Policies to harness the benefits for rural regions
	Self-driving cars	- Shared self-driving cars can improve public transport. - Increasing attractiveness of living in rural regions. - Easier access to services and social networks.	- Ensure good quality broadband connection. - Define regulations for autonomous cars and the low modal share of public transport. - Promote usership rather than ownership. - Improve online-mapping and quality of rural roads.
	3D printers	- Access mass-manufactured goods without waiting for delivery. - Produce goods to sell and adapt to rural industries. - Boost entrepreneurship. - Reduce the market dependence of rural regions on mass-manufactured goods (tools). - Increase the efficiency and autonomy of public services (healthcare inputs).	- Ensure a quality broadband connection. -Train professionals for maintenance and provision. - Disseminate information about technology.
	Drones	- Attract firms to test and conduct research projects with drones. - Improve access to goods (e.g. mass consumption goods, medicines). - Reduce production and delivery costs. - Boost the productivity of rural businesses.	- Ensure a quality broadband connection. - Define regulation and privacy policies. - Incentivise testing and support pilot applications.
	Advanced communications techniques	- Attract and retain workers by improving the teleworking experience. - Enhance social and labour connections. - Allow for collaborative innovation systems among firms and research centres. - Increase the efficiency of rural business and training of workers.	- Ensure a quality broadband connection. - Support firms to invest in data and organisational change to improve teleworking. - Enhance knowledge and information about augmented reality (AR) and virtual reality (VR).
	e-Education	- Enhance traditional learning experiences and make education more accessible and inclusive. - Retain the young population and attract families to settle in more rural areas. - Support reskilling of the workforce to facilitate the shift of economic activity.	- Ensure a quality broadband connection. - Awareness of the benefits of open education at the public and private levels. - Enhance teachers' training and the involvement of academic institutions in technology. - Increase student support (either in person

		- Improve teacher training.	or virtually).
	e-Health	- Increase healthcare coverage and quality in rural regions. - Enhance the skills of medical staff. - Improve information for patients and doctors. - Reduce transport cost in conducting a medical procedure.	- Ensure a quality broadband connection. - Train health professionals. - Conduct awareness campaigns. - Update ICT infrastructure and equipment in hospitals and medical centres.

Source: OECD (2020[37]) *Rural Well-being: Geography of Opportunities*, OECD Rural Studies, OECD Publishing, Paris, https://dx.doi.org/10.1787/d25cef80-en.

In summary

The post COVID-19 scenario is uncertain in many ways, but one thing is likely: the increasing adoption and acceptance of virtual working methods and social interactions. Remote working was a sudden experiment for many actors and involved different challenges for adoption. Yet, results have been rather positive in many aspects, including greenhouse gas emissions, time flexibility, work-life balance and productivity. As a result, in the future, many firms and workers will likely increase the adoption of a hybrid remote working model, compared to the pre-COVID-19 situation.

This new possibility to work and access services remotely will open up many opportunities for places with a low population density to attract new residents and firms. Given that many workers no longer need to go into the office every day, the arguments in favour of leaving big cities are certainly more convincing than before the pandemic. A new set of priorities is taking hold, as the lower living costs and increased affordability of larger spaces in low density regions coupled with greater access to environmental amenities are particularly relevant for firms and people. Either with full-time or a hybrid remote working, firms located in central business districts have incentives to reduce or consolidate office space. This type of change in real estate decisions from the private sector could improve access or affordability of housing and offices in cities.

Yet, a decline of cities is unlikely. Benefits from agglomeration economies will likely be a predominant factor to retain workers and firms in cities. A big exodus from cities would not be desirable for economic, social and environmental aspects. A decline in large urban centres would lead to a loss of economies of scale affecting national growth, efficiency in provision of public services and meeting environmental goals.

This chapter identifies four post-COVID-19 scenarios regarding the impact of remote working on settlement patterns across the territory: i) an important outmigration outside city centres, ii) a movement of actors to the outskirts of cities, iii) a greater attraction of intermediate cities, and iv) little movement but with a hybrid working model. A commonality of these scenarios is the acknowledgement that technology will keep disrupting the way people and businesses interact, which will have an impact (greater or lesser) on spatial distribution and commuting patterns.

Irrespective of the post-pandemic scenario and the decision of workers and firms to relocate across the territory, policies need to be flexible and prepare regions to seize the changes that remote working and other technologies can cause. Indeed, decisions by people and businesses to leave the city entails a cost-benefit analysis, in which local government actions might play a decisive role. Governments need to ensure that people and firms willing to adopt remote working have the right conditions to do so. Therefore the COVID-19 can become a trigger to increase quality of life in rural places, while unlocking and harmonising new growth opportunities throughout the territory.

G7 policies to seize benefits from remote working

The need for remote working during the pandemic led many governments to adapt their policies and regulations to ensure the right conditions and outcomes for workers and firms to benefit from this labour practice. This section discusses policy responses adopted by G7 countries to bolster the benefits and mitigate the challenges of remote working and to attract people and firms that want to further adopt virtual methods of working.

Policies to capture the benefits of remote working for people, places and firms.

Well-designed policies and smarter adoption of remote working could raise workers' well-being and lower firms' costs, while reducing the environmental effects of commuting (OECD, 2020[1]). By working at home, workers can allocate their time efficiently, lower levels of stress related to commuting and save transportation-related resources, while achieving greater overall work-life balance. Yet, as described before, this labour practice can have negative effects in terms of greater cost in utilities - especially in countries with extreme weather (cold winters and hot summers), professional isolation and hidden overtime.

G7 countries, as in many OECD countries, have reacted to the need to increase remote working during the pandemic and implemented a number of policies to make the most of this labour method (Table 4.4). Relevant policies to create the adequate conditions for a wider adoption of efficient remote work can be divided into three main groups i) investment policies, ii) policies to overcome cultural barriers and improve the legal framework and iii) policies to mitigate the potential negative side effects of this labour practice (OECD, 2020[1]).

Complementary investments for remote working

Promoting remote teleworking for all types of sectors and regions requires investments that level the playing field for its adoption. Some of these investments include stimulating investments in high speed broadband, providing financial support to small firms for ICT upgrades and promoting investments in digital skills among workers.

In the short term, all G7 countries have identified ICT support to workers and firms as a cornerstone policy to allow everyone to benefit from remote working. As depicted in Table 4.1, many G7 countries have provided either tax relief (UK, Canada), in-kind services (Italy) or direct grant support (Japan) for workers and SMEs to improve work equipment or technologies. For example, Italy launched the "Digital Solidarity" initiative, a portal where companies (in particular SMEs and self-employed) can access free digital services from large private sector companies (e.g. online conferencing, mobile data, cloud computing, etc.) (OECD, 2020[38]).

In the medium term, a common objective across G7 countries is to improve broadband connectivity in all regions. As discussed in the last section of this chapter, many countries have established strategies to level the playing field in terms of broadband connectivity among urban and non-metropolitan regions. Yet, there is still not a clear focus on ensuring equal internet speeds across the territory.

Overcoming cultural and legal hurdles for remote working

Remote working still faces a number of cultural barriers inside companies and the legal framework has many grey areas with regard to labour security and support for teleworkers. G7 countries have implemented polices to overcome these barriers:

- Promoting a 'right to telework'. G7 countries have taken actions to establish the right of workers to work from home. While it is not a statutory right, most G7 countries had directives even before

COVID-19 to encourage employers to allow employees to work from home wherever possible. In France, the *order of September 2017 to strengthen social dialogue*, which stipulated the right to telework without the need to change labour contracts, had established that in the event of exceptional circumstances (e.g. epidemics), the implementation of teleworking can be considered as necessary.

- Information campaigns on the broader societal benefits of home office. All G7 countries have implemented either information campaigns about the explicit benefits of teleworking, guidelines for workers and managers to best deal with remote working or platforms to resolve questions about remote working (e.g. France).
- Adapting the legal and regulatory system. For example, France introduced the use of digital signatures more broadly in notaries, while Canada's national employment service has an online tool, called "Job Bank", that has changed its website and adapted its services by allowing applicants to specifically search for teleworking opportunities (OECD, 2020[38]).
- Tax regimes and relief to frontier workers has been a major subject during the boom of teleworking. A co-ordinated regulation is necessary to prevent cross-border teleworking from undermining national labour standards and wage agreements (Baldwin, 2019[39]). Some G7 countries have already signed agreements to address this issue:
    - France and Germany along with Belgium and Switzerland have all agreed to lay down specific tax regimes for frontier workers (Ministére des Affaires Étrangeres, 2020[40]).
    - Germany has concluded mutual agreements with Austria, Luxembourg, and the Netherlands on the taxation of frontier workers, stating that the employment income related to work-days spent at home due to COVID-19 can remain taxable in the state where the usual place of work is located.

Mitigate potential side effects of remote working

As previously mentioned, remote working can lead to negative side effects for workers and firms, which can be overcome with policy responses. Workers can face isolation, 'hidden overtime' or increased costs in utilities, while firms can perceive negative effects on innovation, team cohesion and motivation. Policies can help mitigate these effects by promoting opportunities for in-person exchange (e.g. promoting co-working spaces across the country), encouraging the 'right to disconnect' or policies to avoid increased costs related to working space and IT equipment on workers.

G7 countries have implemented policies to address some of these challenges:

- Information campaigns for workers and firms to manage teleworking. This includes encouraging employers to introduce new models to manage employees in remote working. (e.g. Japan has published guidelines for labour management to encourage workers to work from home)
- Promotion of flexible work arrangements to ensure employees have the option to telework. In some countries (France, Germany) collective arrangements have agreed to monitor and reduce hidden overtime when working at home (e.g. in French post and telecom sector)
- Most countries have also set up dedicated programmes to allow workers to deduct higher utility bills from their taxes.

Table 4.6 summarises the main policy responses in G7 countries to facilitate teleworking.

Table 4.4. Remote working policies in G7 countries as a response to the COVID-19 crisis.

Country	Policies (selected)
Canada	• Information campaigns ("Going Remote Guide", "Remote Work Toolkit for Employers from City of Vancouver") • Home office expenses deduction and simplification to claim these expenses on the personal income tax (The Canada Revenue Agency) • Greater resources for community organisations to improve workplace accessibility and access to jobs in response to COVID-19
France	• Accelerate new uses and digital services (trained digital mediators, close to digital places) • National funding to support regional digital projects • Support to national inter-professional agreement between unions and employers which determines that companies cover worker's expenses to perform their tasks under remote working.
Italy	• A ministerial decree to encourage teleworking in the private sector. A plan to move at least 50% of public administration jobs to remote working • A 15% tax credit for investments in technologies (including software) and devices that enable agile work in the "Relaunch Decree" • Necessary IT equipment (laptops and tablets) made available to Public Administration employees (Cura Italia decree)
Germany	• Employees are entitled to deduct up to EUR 600 in home office costs (electricity, heating, etc.) from their income tax in 2020 and 2021 • Claim office expenses recognised for tax purposes as income-related expenses up to the amount of EUR 1 250 in the year of assessment
Japan	• Regional Vitalization Teleworking Grant to local governments • Information campaigns about delocalisation outside cities and new types of management • Access to IT support and management to promote teleworking in SMEs • Broadband investment
UK	• Tax relief to balance additional household costs from teleworking • Broadband investments
United States	• Information campaigns and guidance to firms and workers on remote working or flexible working hours • The U.S. Telework Enhancement Act requires the head of each executive agency to create a policy for their employees' teleworking • Some states announced they won't impose a corporate income tax nexus due to the temporary presence of new teleworkers (District of Columbia, Indiana, North Dakota)

Source: Own elaboration based on OECD (2020[41]) Answers from OECD G7 country delegates to the OECD survey on long-term spatial policy responses to COVID-19

Some policies are actively setting up incentives to attract firms and workers to non-metropolitan regions

Some policy programmes, mainly from regional governments, have created policy strategies to attract workers or firms interested in further adopting remote working. While most G7 countries do not have explicit national policies to drive the relocation decisions of workers, different regional and local governments have established strategies to attract new economic agents to their territory. For most non-metropolitan regions, particularly those remote, digitalisation and attraction policies are a way to tackle depopulation and rapid ageing. As this working method opens up new opportunities for women and people with disabilities to join the labour market (Chapter 2), strategies to attract women and families will help achieve rural revitalisation and build resilient communities.

Some of the strategies to attract workers and firms that adopt remote working include financial or in-kind incentives as well as programmes to ease the relocation process. Financial incentives can be issued to cover the cost of relocation or to sustain the installation during the first few months, while in-kind incentives include providing office space or housing for newcomers. Strategies for easing the relocation can involve offering networking opportunities with local firms and community or creating fast track tools to accelerate the administrative process related to moving into the area:

- **In-kind incentives**. Some regional governments have aimed to improve remote work conditions by providing in-kind facilities for co-working such as industrial parks or co-working spaces. This strategy reduces the cost of offices for newcomers and also creates space for exchanging ideas and agglomeration economies among firms and workers, recreating the in-person contact that cities offer. For example, the Schleswig-Holstein region in Germany launched a pilot initiative, called CoWorkLand, which rezoned empty buildings in rural areas to create co-working spaces as a new solution for workers.
- **Easing the relocation process**. Some local strategies have aimed to promote the benefits of the non-metropolitan regions and to create networks with local actors before their arrival. For example, Gers, France has launched the *SOHO SOLO* initiative to support independent entrepreneurs who wish to settle in the region by discussing in advance practicalities and needs (access to trains and planes or quality and places to educate children) and offering meetings with other workers already in place and sharing the experience of their families (Soho Solo, 2021[42]).
- **Financial support for relocalisation**. Other governments have established active financial support to attract workers (Tusla, Oklahoma or Vermont in US). For example, Tusla, Oklahoma launched the Tulsa Remote initiative which provides remote workers and digital nomads with a maximum USD 10 000 grant (partly upfront for relocation expenses and in the form of a monthly stipend), a one-year membership at a local co-working space, support in finding housing, and regular community-building opportunities (OECD, 2020[38]).
- **Flexible/temporarily attraction of remote workers**. In Japan, prior to COVID-19 some regions were promoting the concept of the "workation" (work + vacation) as a way to encourage longer-term stays among visitors and travellers in non-metropolitan regions, while contributing to a more sustainable regional revitalisation model. After COVID-19, *workation* gained a greater role as a policy strategy and was actively supported by the national government. Regions like Nishi-awa (Tokushima) or Urabandai region (Fukushima) offered plans to remote workers that include working facilities and organised touristic tours.

At the national level, within G7 countries, Japan is an outstanding case of a country with a national strategy promoting teleworking as a tool to reverse the population decline as it seeks to reduce the excessive concentration of the population in the Tokyo metropolitan area and revitalize non-metropolitan economies.

Japan's teleworking policy: an active strategy to balance the distribution of settlements across the territory.

With the COVID-19 pandemic, Japan's government has seen in remote working and digitalisation a possibility to accelerate the goal of tackling population decline and boost quality of life by repopulating non-metropolitan regions in a family-friendly setting with a better work-life balance. The country has long struggled to boost its fertility rate to the replacement level, partially due to the work culture, a deterioration of employment opportunities for young men and the traditional gender division of labour (Tsuya, 2017[43]) Benefiting from the digitalisation trend, the country updated in December 2020 its core policy, which was implemented in 2014, to address population decline and repopulate non-metropolitan regions. *The Comprehensive Strategy for Overcoming the Population Decline and Vitalizing Local Economy* (Box 4.3). Some of the mechanism to promote remote working in this strategy include:

- Provide local governments a grant to enhance local conditions for teleworking practices, including setting up satellite offices in non-metropolitan regions (the Regional Vitalization Teleworking Grant).

- Information campaigns to promote the advantages of remote working for firms and local governments
- Promoting flexible working styles. This includes guidelines for employers to manage teleworkers and update labour practices.
- Specific support to ease implementation of teleworking in SMEs, including grants and free consulting service by IT experts.

This policy goes beyond the support to teleworking and actively incentivise relocation into non-metropolitan regions. In December 2020, The Comprehensive Strategy *for Overcoming the Population Decline* and *Vitalizing Local Economy* was amended by including measures to face the pandemic, such as promoting digital transformation, supporting increased teleworking and the economy decarbonisation. The amended policy strategy stresses the relevance for creating attractive universities and industries in regions, and increasing the number of people who move or visit places outside the capital city. Furthermore, it recognizes the importance of attracting women to revitalize rural areas and build resilient community tools to trigger this relocalisation out of Tokyo by setting up:

- Grants to municipalities (except the ones within Greater Tokyo) that promote teleworking as a regional revitalisation measure such as covering 75% of municipality expenses on systems for satellite offices of companies and shared office spaces (Government of Japan, 2021[44]),
- A national programme to match businesses with municipalities looking to accept branch offices, and
- An enhanced subsidy programme that financially supports people who live or work in central Tokyo and will move to work in non-metropolitan regions. This grant target people or families who move outside Tokyo to raise their children or take care of elderly family members, while continuing to work for their employers in Tokyo through remote work (The Japanese Cabinet Secretariat and the Cabinet Office, 2020[45]).

Box 4.3. Japan's policy strategy to overcome overconcentration

Japan is one of the world's super-aging societies and faces a rapid population decline. To solve this issue, In 2014, the Japanese government set up a policy to revitalize the local economy and attain a goal of keeping the population above 100 million by 2060 (Today's population is 126 million). Two specific strategies define this policy:

- The "Long-term Vision for Overcoming the Population Decline and Vitalizing Local Economy in Japan". This strategy sets Japan's vision to alleviate the rapid population decline and revitalize the regional economy by 2060. The primary goals are: 1) Ease the overconcentration in Greater Tokyo Area; 2) Support the younger generation's desire to work, marry, and have children; and 3) Solve the regional challenges based on the specific characteristics of each region. This strategy is revised every five years.
- The "Comprehensive Strategy for Overcoming the Population Decline and Vitalizing Local Economy in Japan". This sets Japan's basic policy principles and its implementation for the coming five years. The objectives are: 1) Generate stable employment in all regions, 2) Create a new inflow of people to regions, 3) Facilitate young people's wish to marry, have children, and become parents, and 4) Create regional areas suited to modern times, preserve safe and secure living conditions, and promote co-operation between regions. This strategy is revised every year.

The government and local governments co-operate in solving issues by: 1) creating a "Regional Economy Data Analysis System" to provide local governments with big data to analyse various indicators, including demographics, business activities, and tourism trends in each region; 2) providing financial support (grant for local governments, local allocation tax, and tax incentives for businesses) to create the "Regional Comprehensive Strategy" in each region and its implementation; 3) supporting local government's capacity by assigning government officials and other experts to assist and provide consultancy services to governments of smaller municipalities.

Source: Cabinet Secretariat of Japan (2014[46]), Regional Empowerment for Japan's Growth.

Cities are also adapting to become better places to live and work

Long-term city policy responses to COVID-19 have highlighted the relevance of transformations towards inclusive, green and smart cities (OECD, 2020[47]). Policies around these three goals would help large cities to remain attractive and retain workers or firms that might be tempted to perform their economic activity remotely elsewhere.

Offering affordable and adequate housing is one of the chief policy targets to make cities more inclusive. Most of the world's metropolitan areas have experienced faster population growth in the commuting zone than in the city, partly as a consequence of a shortage of housing availability in the city itself (OECD/European Commission, 2020[21]). As a consequence of COVID-19, some cities have adapted their housing policies to reduce commuting times, increase available housing and create inclusive neighbourhoods. For example, Vienna (Austria) has announced important housing developments disseminated around the city in attractive residential environments at an affordable price for citizens of different income levels (OECD, 2020[47]).

Offering environmental amenities and improving urban mobility are also the focus of many city governments. Cities are adapting urban design and reclaiming public space to ensure easier access to services and amenities. For example, greater investments in bicycle infrastructure, concepts such as the "15 minute city" (ensuring access to essential functions in a short perimeter) or pedestrianisation of streets are policies that have gained traction, with the aim is to improve mobility and well-being for citizens (OECD, 2021[48]). Other policies are looking at opportunities to replace abandoned buildings or public spaces to create parks and green areas.

Cities are also increasingly embracing digitalisation and smart tools to improve citizens' lives, including greater security, access to services and political participation. Digitalisation of municipal services accompanied with interventions to improve digital skills are core policies for many cities (e.g., Milan, Italy).

This pandemic could also accelerate urban regeneration policies in cities to expand supply of housing and community areas. For example, the Tokyo Metropolitan Government has a project to give grants to private companies to renovate abandoned buildings and transform them into 1) houses for parents who take care of children, 2) houses for single parents, 3) houses for foreign workers, 4) community spaces (e.g. places for communicating between parents, event spaces, places for elderly people to eat together) (Tokyo Metropolitan Government, 2020[49]).

It is worth noting that countries have also developed specific policies to increase the attractiveness of intermediate cities (those with 50 000 to 500 000 people), which have received renewed attention, as they are at the core of territorial recovery but their potential is often underexploited. These cities can provide a good compromise of high quality of life with sufficient critical mass to achieve agglomeration benefits, while playing an important role for the surrounding territories. Yet, they experience difficulties in attractiveness, degraded housing or commercial vitality. France, for example, created a programme called *Action cœur de ville* (action in the heart of the city) to finance projects to revitalise medium-sized cities (e.g. improving housing in the city centre and accessibility and transport).

Policy takeaways

Policies that encourage people and firm's mobility can struggle to produce sustainable changes in territories. Subsidies or grants for people to relocate can create incentives to obtain the short-term economic benefit, instead of increasing long-term attractiveness of places. Without the right conditions at the local level (e.g. access to services), these policies risk to have little benefit in relation to the cost, as firms tend to be more responsive to co-location externalities rather than subsidies (Ascani, Crescenzi and Iammarino, 2016[50]; Devereux, Griffith and Simpson, 2007[51]). If not well-planed, moves might also lead to declines in welfare for existing residents, for example by increasing housing costs and a reduced capacity for public services. Furthermore, given the high share of elderly population living in Tokyo, policies inducing movement can struggle to trigger commuting of older workers, as age correlates negatively with mobility (OECD, 2020[37]).

Competition among regions for workers and firms can create spatial distortions and lead to aggregate inefficiencies within a country (Lingwen Zheng and Warner, 2010[52]). In the extreme case, increasing regional competition to attract economic actors through tax incentives or grants could lead to the "race to the bottom" scenario where local governments decrease their fiscal net revenue and end up with under provision of public goods for local communities (Glaeser, 2001[53]). Local tax incentives or grants for firms or workers to relocate to a region can also create distortions with local firms and workers.

National governments should help co-ordinate regional attraction policies and support broader strategies that improve the enabling factors for a sustainable development in regions. Balancing economic growth across types of regions should, instead, rely on place-based intervention that targets places with less focus on people or firm-based identifiers (Yagan et al., 2014[54]). Investing in quality broadband and access to health and education are some areas that can increase long-term attractiveness in regions.

Enabling factors to make non-metropolitan regions attractive places for people and firms

The boom in remote working and digitalisation of economic activities ushered in by the COVID-19 pandemic revealed the need to increase the structural attractiveness of non-metropolitan regions for people (workers and their families as well as young people and retirees) and businesses. Most non-metropolitan regions of the OECD and G7 face greater population decline and rapid ageing than metropolitan regions (OECD, 2020[37]). Furthermore, their economic performance in terms of GDP per capita, productivity and employment rates is on average below those in metropolitan regions, which has expanded regional inequality in almost all OECD countries since the 2008 financial crisis (OECD, 2020[37]). This section outlines the policies from G7 countries to increase the long-term attractiveness of non-metropolitan regions by improving access to fast broadband, high quality healthcare and education.

Government strategies to improve digitalisation in non-metropolitan regions

Without policy intervention, the effects of digitalisation could further increase the well-being and economic gap between non-metropolitan and metropolitan regions. Non-metropolitan regions tend to have outdated ICT infrastructures and deployments of new technologies (e.g. 5G) are more likely to occur first in urban regions as the high population density makes these investments more profitable. Increasing digital capacity and skills is also a pivotal competitive factor for places to succeed.

Digitalisation can help non-metropolitan regions enhance growth opportunities and quality of life. Digitalisation can increase job and market opportunities (e-commerce) and new technologies (e.g. drones, automotive vehicles) reduce transport times and costs. Digitalisation can also enhance well-being, living standards, access to quality healthcare and education, innovations to accelerate environmental sustainability, and equal opportunity (OECD, 2020[37]). By embracing digitalisation, rural areas and towns can strengthen their resilience against future shocks and tap into megatrends (demographic change, digitalisation and climate change). G7 governments have acknowledged this issue and implemented some policy responses to strengthen digitalisation in non-metropolitan regions.

Digitalisation contributes to making non-metropolitan areas economically competitive and increasing well-being

The pandemic has exacerbated the existing digital urban-rural divide. The persistent gap in broadband accessibility between non-metropolitan and cities is more evident when comparing accessibility to high speed internet (OECD, 2020[37]). For example in Canada, internet performance testing found that median download speeds for rural Canadians (5.62 Mbps) were approximately 10 times slower than for urban Canadians (51.54 Mbps) (CIRA, 2020[55]). While urban internet speeds have nearly doubled since the beginning of the pandemic, rural speeds have plateaued. Furthermore, people in non-metropolitan regions have lower digital skills.

All G7 countries have implemented a type of policy to enhance digitalisation in non-metropolitan regions. Common policies ensure non-metropolitan regions have high-quality broadband so communities have access to services (telemedicine). They have also established and prepared places for teleworking in non-metropolitan regions (Italy, Japan). Others have actively supported digital transformation in local governments (Italy, Japan). Many governments are still investing in civil infrastructure (e.g., telecommunications infrastructure and roads) to strengthen accessibility and mobility for rural economies (Canada, Italy).

Table 4.5. Selected policies of G7 countries to improve digital connectivity in all regions

Countries	Policies
Canada	• Funding project to provide high-speed internet connectivity (Connecting Canadians programme Universal Broadband Fund and CRTC Broadband Fund, Southwestern Integrated Fibre Technology (SWIFT) project in Ontario) • Ensuring the deployment of broadband infrastructure in rural areas (Southwestern Integrated Fibre Technology (SWIFT) • Support small and medium-sized enterprises to embrace digital technologies (Ontario) (Digital Main Street Platform) and provides relief grants to small businesses for developing a website or e-commerce capabilities (Canada United Small Business Relief Fund)
France	• the National Broadband Plan, which extends fibre optics to subscribers throughout the country by 2025 • France Very High Speed (Très Haut Débit) which aims to give all French people access to good broadband (minimum 8 Mbit / s) and a very high speed internet connection (minimum 30 Mbit / s) by the end of 2022 • The creation of 4 000 digital mediator positions that provide digital mediation and support to users of digital technology, addressing its challenges for a large part of French people living in remote areas
Italy	• The Recovery Fund (or Next Generation EU), which is used for the development of network infrastructures • Installation and activation of satellite offices and modems for internet connection via satellite in rural areas of Piedmont and the purchase of decoders, antennas and all the material that can be used to install a satellite system to surf the internet from home and other places • Relaunch strategy for Inner Areas to strategies for localisation of production and job creation, including supporting digital transformation "(Piano Sud 2030")
Germany	• "German Gigabit programme", which finances broadband in areas where there is no market-driven expansion • State subsidies for fibre optic network expansion • European Agricultural Fund for Rural Development (EAFRD), the European Regional Development Fund (ERDF) and the joint task "Improving the Regional Economic Structure" (GRW) funded broadband expansion projects
Japan	• Improving ICT equipment such as 5G fibre optic communications (Box 4.5) • The government supports technology development, IT investment, and markets for small and medium-

Countries	Policies
	sized enterprises • The government provides digital specialists from private sectors to regional areas to share their skills with local governments
UK	• Gigabit Broadband Voucher Scheme (GBVS) and the Scottish Broadband Voucher Scheme (SBVS), which fund the cost of installing gigabit-capable broadband in rural areas
United States	• The U.S. Department of Agriculture (USDA)'s ReConnect programme, which aimed at increasing broadband development in rural areas through grants, loans and combinations • Rural Digital Opportunity Fund (RDOF), which improves connectivity in rural areas (2019) • American Broadband Initiative (ABI), which increases efficiency in government broadband programmes

Source: Own elaboration based on OECD (2020[41]) Answers from OECD G7 country delegates to the OECD survey on long-term spatial policy responses to COVID-19.

Box 4.4. Canada's policy to strengthen digitalisation

Canada has set strengthening rural broadband policies as one of its key challenges because of its low population density for many years. Several different federal governments have provided subsidies to service providers in an effort to have them improve the connectivity in these areas. For example, the Government of Canada has accelerated the budget project in 2019 and will support the Universal Broadband Fund (UBF) to deploy large-scale broadband projects in rural and remote communities.

The Government of Canada, in collaboration with the Government of Ontario, launched the construction of broadband infrastructure (December 9, 2020) to deliver reliable internet access to nearly all citizens.

The Government of Canada and the Government of Québec launched the Québec haut débit program to provide help to connect 230 000 households and enterprises in rural communities to high-speed Internet.

A wide range of policies have been designed to assist individuals, families, businesses, and industries in rural areas, including helping businesses to adopt new technologies to overcome this pandemic and increase the attractiveness of these areas.

Source: OECD, (2021[56]), Delivering Quality Education and Health Care to All: Preparing Regions for Demographic Change, OECD Rural Studies; OECD (2020[41]), *Answers from OECD G7 country delegates to the OECD survey on long-term spatial policy responses to COVID-19.*

Box 4.5. Japan's policy to strengthen digitalisation

Digital transformation can contribute to resolving various challenges in regions while improving productivity and convenience, which will enhance the quality of industry and people's lives. Also, Japan faces an aging society, especially in rural areas, and the number of labourers and markets is shrinking. It is important to create a strong economy in rural areas and create jobs. The pandemic reveals the delay of digitalisation in the national and local governments. In non-metropolitan regions, it is important to improve digitalisation to increase their attractiveness.

- Improving ICT equipment such as 5G. In 2020, 5G service started in Japan. The government assists ICT companies in developing 5G base stations and fibre optic communications in rural areas. This enables efficient and advanced services and helps people receive the same level of services in each rural region (e.g. online education and online medical treatments) regardless of location.
- Supporting local enterprises by digitalisation. To improve productivity in rural areas, the government supports the development of technology, IT investment, and markets, which strengthens the competitiveness of local industries. The government helps specific industries in regions such as manufacturing, agriculture, and tourism invest in capital (the industries are determined on a region-by-region basis). In addition to this, the government encourages rural regions to create innovation by supporting co-operation between local industries and universities. Further, it will improve the financial environment by encouraging small and medium-sized enterprises to co-operate, which enables these companies to challenge their business innovation.
- Developing human resources. The government provides digital specialists from private sectors to regional areas to share their skills with local governments and have webinars about how to incorporate digital technologies into the local policy for revitalising the local economy, enhancing to create educational projects to developing experts for using digital technology.
- Promoting the use of new technologies. The government promotes the uptake of new technologies (AI, drones, 5G, edge computing, self-driving technologies, etc.) by informing good practices.

Source: Cabinet Secretariat of Japan (2020[57]) the Comprehensive Strategy for Overcoming the Population Decline and Vitalizing Local Economy in Japan.

Policy takeaways

G7 policies to expand broadband coverage are headed in the right direction, but preparing non-metropolitan regions for future digitalisation trends require a more active approach. In turn, this will ensure everyone has access to high quality broadband while helping to improve digital skills. To this end, governments should:

- Accelerate equal access to high quality and affordable communication services in non-metropolitan regions by:
  - Implementing holistic policies that foster competition in communication markets to increase investments and reduce prices for communication services
  - Reducing barriers to broadband deployment with simplified licensing procedures, streamlined access to rights of way and faster permits

- Creating funding methods to increase connectivity, including demand aggregation models to ensure financial viability of projects, public private partnership (PPP) initiatives and coverage obligations in spectrum auctions.
- Implement educational and training programmes to boost digital skills of all communities and firms outside metropolitan regions. This includes implementing courses on basic use of ICT technologies and computers, and capacity building on software and ICT maintenance.

Improving access to basic services (education and health) will increase non-metropolitan regions' attractiveness

The COVID-19 pandemic revealed some of the difficulties of people in non-metropolitan regions to access health and social care services. Geographical distances and less developed transportation services exacerbate the challenge to provide public services. Non-metropolitan regions also tend to face an increasing number of closures of hospitals and the consolidation of schools, due to increasing depopulation and limited local revenues (OECD, 2020[37]). Furthermore, social isolation, a lack of medical staff, and an aging population are particular challenges for non-metropolitan regions (OECD, 2021[56]).

Digitalisation has proven to be a useful tool to improve delivery of health and education. Health technology and innovation are changing how doctors and hospital staff tackle clinical and health problems. These tools let clinics change the procedures and practical styles for delivering healthcare through technologies such as process innovations, e-Health, and Big Data. Good internet access, access to equipment, and use of online distance learning platforms are crucial factors to determine who benefits and who suffers from online education.

G7 countries have already implemented a number of policies to enhance education access through digitalisation (Table 4.6). Most countries support e-learning at school by providing equipment such as laptops, tablets, and SIM cards (Canada, France, Italy, Germany, Japan and the US). Furthermore, countries like Canada leverage ICT to foster social innovation through the collaboration with communities in primary and secondary schools, while expanding co-operation with private companies to increase e-education (OECD, 2021[56]).

In terms of health, most G7 countries have taken measures to reap the benefits of e-health (Table 4.7). This includes investing in infrastructure capacity to support online treatment (Canada, Japan, US), or ease regulatory barriers to encourage the use of teleconsultation (France, Germany, Japan, UK, US) (OECD, 2021[56]). Moreover, some non-metropolitan regions have implemented mobile health clinics to guarantee adequate primary care (Germany).

Table 4.6. Selected policies of G7 countries to provide online education in all regions

Country	Policies
Canada	• "Broadband Modernisation Programme (2020-21)" for e-learning (Ontario) • The project "Networked Schools", a school for e-learning (Quebec) • Partnership with Apple and Rogers Telecommunications to provide low-income students with iPads and free mobile data plans (Ontario)
France	• Digital plan for education, which enables 500 schools to be connected to the internet and access to tablets or laptops
Italy	• Tax deductions (up to 30%) for the donation of IT equipment to enable students to access distance learning • Contribution for the purchase/rental of equipment dedicated to support secondary schools (Lazio, 2020) • Inner Areas National Strategy, which aims to contribute to improving their inhabitants' well-being and quality of life (education and healthcare) in rural areas (2014). This is funded by the European Regional Development Fund (ERDF), the European Social Fund (ESF), and the European Agricultural Fund for Rural Development (EAFRD). • The "Territorial Strategy" aims to improve access to and quality of essential services such as transportation, health and education.

Country	Policies
Germany	• Budget project, which equips more than 40 000 schools and colleges with faster internet, wireless access points and tablet computers
Japan	• The "Giga School project" provides school children with fast internet connection and equipment in schools
UK	• Government-funded support for setting up a digital education platform for schools
United States	• the CARES Act Elementary and Secondary School Emergency Relief Fund, which financially supports schools and ensures the proper functioning of online education during the pandemic • Coronavirus Aid, Relief and Economic Security (CARES) Act, which support a distance learning and telemedicine programme

Source: Own elaboration based on OECD (2020[41]) Answers from OECD G7 country delegates to the OECD survey on long-term spatial policy responses to COVID-19

Table 4.7. Selected policies of G7 countries to provide e-health in all regions

Country	Policies
Canada	• High-speed broadband internet in schools and the delivery of well-being and mental health services (The 2016 budget -Ontario) • Ontario Telemedicine Network (2017)
Italy	• Inner Areas National Strategy to improve inhabitants' quality of life for example on access to education and healthcare (funded by European funds). • Improving access to and quality of essential services such as transportation, health and education (The "Territorial Strategy")
Germany	• Developing a network to combat disease and early prevention, including cancer and digitalisation of healthcare provision (Global Health Hub Germany)
Japan	• Promoting online healthcare treatments
UK	• Tax benefit for companies in the digital health and care sector
United States	• Medicare investment on telemedicine services • Coronavirus Aid, Relief and Economic Security (CARES) Act, to support a telemedicine programme

Source: Own elaboration based on OECD (2020[41]) Answers from OECD G7 country delegates to the OECD survey on long-term spatial policy responses to COVID-19

Countries have also implemented a number of strategies to improve overall access to services in regions. Improving accessibility to a greater range of amenities can help attract a broader range of population. Cultural and leisure amenities can be prioritised by the younger population, while elderly care facilities can attract retirees and senior citizens. Of chief importance in the post-COVID-19 scenario and in countries facing rapid ageing, like Japan, is to focus on strategies that improve quality of life for the entire family. Childcare facilities for example can help people found families , while lowering the trade-off for women to integrate the labour market.

Some policies across OECD countries, including G7 countries, offer good practices to support child and elderly care in non-metropolitan regions. Extended schools programmes are strategies that encourage schools to offer a wider set of services, including support for parents and childcare (UK). Multi-function centres can also be a good solution to attain efficiency and economies of scale in the provision of different services under a single management structure, including kindergarten or day care services, pre-primary and primary education, and a community facility (Japan, Lithuania) (OECD, 2021[56]). Strategies to attract healthcare workers to low density populated areas are a common policy target in many countries. Regarding elderly care, many countries try to increase and retain the number of caregivers, by giving financial support for their training programmes and using public image campaigns, increasing wages, and providing counselling services to caregivers (France, Japan, the UK, the US) (OECD, 2020[58]).

Policy takeaways

Despite the policy effort of governments to improve the quality of public service delivery in non-metropolitan regions, there is room for improvement on a number of fronts, including addressing skill and physical infrastructure gaps. The OECD (2021[56]) has identified a number of policies that help governments prepare non-metropolitan regions for future changes related to demographics and digitalisation:

- Increasing scale on the provision of education, health and government services in non-metropolitan regions, which includes:
    - regarding education: developing school clusters or structures in which schools formally co-operate under a single leadership to allocate resources more flexibly and efficiently. Furthermore, taking a flexible approach when considering class sizes and regulatory matters will benefit education in scarcely-populated areas
    - regarding health: providing incentives for the establishment of multi-disciplinary health centres and reinforcing primary and integrated care provision in non-metropolitan regions as it is generally the first point of contact for the majority of patients' needs
- Strengthening policies for attracting, retaining and empowering teachers and health workers
- Promoting a greater use of digitalisation to provide services in non-metropolitan regions, which includes:
    - Investing in managing and operating software and improving intellectual property and security protocols
    - Enhancing co-operation between schools/healthcare centres and ICT firms
    - Improving ICT training to teachers, healthcare and local government staff
- To support equal opportunities in the adoption of remote working, policies could also adapt support services so women, youth and low-skilled can work remotely. This could entail enhancing child and elderly care amenities in non-metropolitan regions and supporting co-working spaces to offer quality work conditions and networking opportunities.

References

Alexander W. Bartik, M. (2020), "How Are Small Businesses Adjusting to COVID-19? Early Evidence from a Survey", *National Bureau of Economic Research*, https://www.nber.org/papers/w26989. [71]

Alexander W. Bartik, Z. (2020), *What Jobs are Being Done at Home During the Covid-19 Crisis? Evidence from Firm-Level Surveys*, https://www.nber.org/papers/w27422 (accessed on 14 February 2021). [70]

Althoff, L. et al. (2020), *The City Paradox: Skilled Services and Remote Work*, Munich Society for the Promotion of Economic Research - CESifo. [36]

Ascani, A., R. Crescenzi and S. Iammarino (2016), "Economic Institutions and the Location Strategies of European Multinationals in their Geographic Neighborhood", *Economic Geography*, Vol. 92/4, pp. 401-429, http://dx.doi.org/10.1080/00130095.2016.1179570. [50]

Baldwin, R. (2019), *The Globotics Upheaval*, Oxford University Press. [39]

Barrero, J., N. Bloom and S. Davis (2020), *Why Working From Home Will Stick*, University of Chicago, Becker Friedman Institute for Economics. [5]

BCG (2020), *What 12,000 Employees Have to Say About the Future of Remote Work*, https://www.bcg.com/publications/2020/valuable-productivity-gains-covid-19 (accessed on 15 January 2021). [20]

BCG, B. (2020), *COVID-19 Employee Sentiment Survey*, https://www.bcg.com/publications/2020/valuable-productivity-gains-covid-19 (accessed on 2021 February 25). [6]

Bloom, N. (2015), "Does working from home work? Evidence from a Chinese experiment.", *The Quarterly Journal of Economics*, Vol. 130(1), pp. 165-218, https://academic.oup.com/qje/article/130/1/165/2337855?login=true. [4]

Cabinet Secretariat of Japan (2020), *Comprehensive Strategy for Overcoming the Population Decline and Vitalizing Local Economy in Japan*. [57]

Cabinet Secretariat of Japan (2014), *Regional Empowerment for Japan's Growth*. [46]

CIRA (2020), *New internet performance data shows urban speeds improving while rural speeds plateau*, https://www.cira.ca/newsroom/state-internet/new-internet-performance-data-shows-urban-speeds-improving-while-rural (accessed on 4 March 2021). [55]

City of Vancouver (2020), *Remote and Flexible Work Toolkit for Employers*, https://vancouver.ca/files/cov/remote-work-toolkit.pdf. [59]

Corriere della Sera (2020), *Smart working, adesso si fa sul serio ma a chi conviene tra capi, dipendenti e aziende?*, https://www.corriere.it/sette/attualita/20_giugno_12/smart-working-adesso-si-fa-serio-ma-chi-conviene-capi-dipendenti-aziende-5fd07e08-abe8-11ea-822f-b27e74f859d1.shtml (accessed on 10 February 2021). [16]

Credit Suisse (2020), *COVID-19 boosts demand for central locations*, http://file:///C:/Users/Sanabria_a/Downloads/swiss-office-property-market-2021-en.pdf. [26]

Devereux, M., R. Griffith and H. Simpson (2007), "Firm location decisions, regional grants and agglomeration externalities", *Journal of Public Economics*, Vol. 91/3-4, pp. 413-435, http://dx.doi.org/10.1016/j.jpubeco.2006.12.002. [51]

Emanuel, N. and E. Harrington (2020), *"Working remotely? : Selection, treatment and the market provision remote work"*, https://scholar.harvard.edu/files/eharrington/files/remote_work.pdf. [3]

Etheridge, B., Y. Wang and L. Tang (2020), *Worker productivity during lockdown and working from home: evidence from self-reports*, https://www.iser.essex.ac.uk/research/publications/working-papers/iser/2020-12. [8]

EUROSTAT (2021), *Work from home, from an external site or on the move*, http://appsso.eurostat.ec.europa.eu/nui/show.do?dataset=isoc_iw_hem&lang=en (accessed on 2021 February 26). [63]

Glaeser, E. (2001), "The Economics Of Location-Based Tax Incentives", *SSRN Electronic Journal*, http://dx.doi.org/10.2139/ssrn.289834. [53]

Glaeser, E. and J. Gottlieb (2009), "The Wealth of Cities: Agglomeration Economies and Spatial Equilibrium in the United States", *Journal of Economic Literature*, https://www.jstor.org/stable/40651531?seq=1#metadata_info_tab_contents. [22]

Gorlick, A. (2020), *The productivity pitfalls of working from home in the age of COVID-19, Stanford News*, https://news.stanford.edu/2020/03/30/productivity-pitfalls-working-home-age-covid-19/. [2]

Government of Japan (2021), *Foundation of the teleworking grants for rural areas*, https://www.kantei.go.jp/jp/singi/sousei/meeting/telework_suishin_kentoukaigi/r3-01-18.html. [44]

H.Dang, H. and C. Nguyencd (2021), "Gender inequality during the COVID-19 pandemic: Income, expenditure, savings, and job loss", *World Development*, https://www.sciencedirect.com/science/article/pii/S0305750X2030423X. [67]

Harris Interactive (2020), *Coronavirus Updated and Research*, https://harris-interactive.co.uk/covid-19/ (accessed on 2 March 2021). [11]

IAB-Forum (2020), *https://www.iab-forum.de/en/the-impact-of-the-covid-19-pandemic-evidence-from-a-new-establishment-survey/*, http://The impact of the Covid-19 pandemic: evidence from a new establishment survey (accessed on 4 February 2021). [14]

IAO (2020), *The coronavirus home office survey: How well are we working from home?*, https://www.iao.fraunhofer.de/en/press-and-media/latest-news/the-coronavirus-home-office-survey-how-well-are-we-working-from-home.html (accessed on 3 January 2021). [13]

Immobiliare (2020), *AUMENTANO LE RICHIESTE DI CASE IN CAMPAGNA*, https://www.immobiliare.it/news/aumentano-le-richieste-di-case-in-campagna-46397/ (accessed on 8 March 2021). [31]

Indeed (2021), *The Office is Not Dead: Most Remote Job Postings Describe Remote Work as 'Temporary'*, https://www.hiringlab.org/uk/blog/2021/03/10/the-office-is-not-dead/ (accessed on 12 March 2021). [10]

JRC, J. (2020), *Telework in the EU before and after the COVID-19: where we were*, https://ec.europa.eu/jrc/sites/jrcsh/files/jrc120945_policy_brief_-_covid_and_telework_final.pdf (accessed on 2021 February 26). [62]

Lanari, C. (2020), *Investireoggi*, https://www.investireoggi.it/economia/smart-working-no-south-working-come-cambia-il-lavoro-con-le-citta-svuotate/ (accessed on 8 March 2021). [30]

Le ministère de l'Économie, des Finances et de la Relance (2020), *Plan de Relance*, https://www.economie.gouv.fr/plan-de-relance. [60]

Lingwen Zheng and M. Warner (2010), "Business Incentive Use Among U.S. Local Governments: A Story of Accountability and Policy Learning", *Economic Development Quarterly*, Vol. 24/4, pp. 325-336, http://dx.doi.org/10.1177/0891242410376237. [52]

Liu, S. and Y Su (2020), *The impact of the COVID-19 pandemic on the demand for density: Evidence from the US housing market.* [24]

LSE Business Review (2020), *Remote working: here to stay?*, http://eprints.lse.ac.uk/104509/1/businessreview_2020_04_02_remote_working_here_to.pdf (accessed on 12 March 2021). [69]

McKinsey & Company (2020), *What's next for remote work: An analysis of 2,000 tasks, 800 jobs, and nine countries*, https://www.mckinsey.com/featured-insights/future-of-work/whats-next-for-remote-work-an-analysis-of-2000-tasks-800-jobs-and-nine-countries (accessed on 2 March 2021). [15]

Ministére des Affaires Étrangeres (2020), *COVID-19 : situation des travailleurs frontaliers*, https://de.ambafrance.org/COVID-19-situation-des-travailleurs-frontaliers. [40]

Ministero dell'Economia e delle Finanze (2020), *COVID-19*, https://www.mef.gov.it/covid-19/I-provvedimenti-del-Governo-a-sostegno-del-Lavoro/. [61]

Ministry of Land, Infrastructure, Transport and Tourism of Japan (2020), *Presentation on changes during COVID-19*, Prepared from "Report on Internal Migration of the Basic Resident Registration" (MIC). [25]

MLIT (2020), *Questionnaire on remote working conducted to enterprises headquartered in Tokyo (August 2020).* [33]

MLIT (2020), *Questionnaire on remote working conducted to workers in Tokyo (August 2020).* [34]

Morikawa, M. (2020), ""Productivity of Working from Home during the COVID-19 Pandemic: Evidence from an Employee Survey"", *Covid Economics*, Vol. 40, pp. 132–147. [9]

Newman, P. (2006), "The environmental impact of cities", *Environment & Urbanization*, http://dx.doi.org/10.1177/0956247806069599. [64]

Newman, P. and J. Kenworthy (2000), "Sustainability and cities: overcoming automobile dependence", *Island press.* [35]

Notaires-Insee (2021), *Indices Notaires-Insee des prix des logements anciens - quatrième trimestre 2020*, https://www.insee.fr/fr/statistiques/5058675#graphique-ipla-g2-fr. [28]

OECD (2021), *Delivering Quality Education and Health Care to All: Preparing Regions for Demographic Change*, OECD Rural Studies, OECD Publishing, Paris, https://dx.doi.org/10.1787/83025c02-en. [56]

OECD (2021), *OECD Regional Outlook 2021*, OECD, http://dx.doi.org/10.1787/17017efe-en. [48]

OECD (2020), *Answers from OECD G7 country delegates to the OECD survey on long-term spatial policy responses to COVID-19.* [41]

OECD (2020), "Exploring policy options on teleworking: Steering local economic and employment development in the time of remote work", *OECD Local Economic and Employment Development (LEED) Papers*, No. 2020/10, OECD Publishing, Paris, https://dx.doi.org/10.1787/5738b561-en. [38]

OECD (2020), *OECD Policy Responses to Coronavirus (COVID-19). Cities policy responses. Updated 23 July 2020*, http://www.oecd.org/coronavirus/policy-responses/cities-policy-responses-fd1053ff/#part-d1e2443. [47]

OECD (2020), *Productivity gains from teleworking in the post COVID-19 era : How can public policies make it happen?*, https://www.oecd.org/coronavirus/policy-responses/productivity-gains-from-teleworking-in-the-post-covid-19-era-a5d52e99/. [1]

OECD (2020), *Productivity gains from teleworking in the post COVID-19 era: How can public policies make it happen?*, https://read.oecd-ilibrary.org/view/?ref=135_135250-u15liwp4jd&title=Productivity-gains-from-teleworking-in-the-post-COVID-19-era (accessed on 2021 March 01). [65]

OECD (2020), *Rural Well-being: Geography of Opportunities*, OECD Rural Studies, OECD Publishing, Paris, https://dx.doi.org/10.1787/d25cef80-en. [37]

OECD (2020), *Who Cares? Attracting and Retaining Care Workers for the Elderly*, OECD Health Policy Studies, OECD Publishing, Paris, https://dx.doi.org/10.1787/92c0ef68-en. [58]

OECD (Forthcoming), *Regional Outlook.* [66]

OECD/European Commission (2020), *Cities in the World: A New Perspective on Urbanisation*, OECD Urban Studies, OECD Publishing, Paris, https://dx.doi.org/10.1787/d0efcbda-en. [21]

Office for National Statistics UK (2020), *Coronavirus and homeworking in the UK: April 2020*, https://www.ons.gov.uk/employmentandlabourmarket/peopleinwork/employmentandemployeetypes/bulletins/coronavirusandhomeworkingintheuk/april2020 (accessed on 13 February 2021). [18]

Ozimek, A. (2020), *The Future of Remote Work*, https://www.upwork.com/press/releases/the-future-of-remote-work (accessed on 14 February 2021). [17]

PWC (2021), *It's time to reimagine where and how work will get done*, https://www.pwc.com/us/en/library/covid-19/us-remote-work-survey.html (accessed on 3 March 2021). [19]

PWC (2021), *PwC's US Remote Work Survey*, https://www.pwc.com/us/en/library/covid-19/us-remote-work-survey.html. [32]

Ramani, A. and N. Bloom (2021), *The doughnut effect of COVID-19 on cities*, https://voxeu.org/article/doughnut-effect-covid-19-cities. [23]

SGV (2020), *Lockdown led to big increase in worker productivity*, https://www.swissinfo.ch/eng/lockdown-led-to-big-jump-in-worker-productivity/45818576 (accessed on 14 February 2021). [72]

Soho Solo (2021), *Le Gers votre nouvel space de travail*, https://www.soho-solo-gers.com/ (accessed on March 2021). [42]

Statistics Canada (2020), *Canadian Survey on Business Conditions: Impact of COVID-19 on businesses in Canada, May 2020*, https://www150.statcan.gc.ca/n1/daily-quotidien/200714/dq200714a-eng.htm (accessed on 4 February 2021). [12]

The Guardian (2021), *Environment*, https://www.theguardian.com/environment/2020/dec/11/rebound-in-carbon-emissions-expected-in-2021-after-fall-caused-by-covid (accessed on 8 March 2021). [68]

The Japanese Cabinet Secretariat and the Cabinet Office (2020), *Grant for relocation*, https://www.kantei.go.jp/jp/singi/sousei/ijyu_shienkin.html. [45]

Tobias, P. and E. Pinto (2020), *The Great American Land Rush of 2020*, https://www.aei.org/research-products/report/the-great-american-land-rush-of-2020/ (accessed on 8 March 2021). [29]

Tokyo Metropolitan Government (2020), *Reiwa 2nd Area Renovation Promotion Support Project*, https://www.metro.tokyo.lg.jp/tosei/hodohappyo/press/2020/08/31/09.html (accessed on March 2021). [49]

Tsuya, N. (2017), *LOW FERTILITY IN JAPAN—NO END IN SIGHT*, Honolulu: East-West Center. [43]

UK HPI (2021), *UK House Price Index for December 2020*, https://www.gov.uk/government/news/uk-house-price-index-for-december-2020. [27]

Yagan, D. et al. (2014), "Moving to opportunity? Migratory insurance over the Great Recession", https://eml.berkeley.edu/~yagan/MigratoryInsurance.pdf (accessed on 27 June 2019). [54]

YouGov, USA TODAY & LinkedIn (2020), *The biggest challenges facing those working from home*, https://eu.usatoday.com/story/money/2020/05/04/coronavirus-pandemic-might-game-changer-working-home/3061862001/ (accessed on 14 February 2021). [7]

Note

[1] These studies analysed productivity on samples of 3 063 and 15 000 employees respectively from one particular working sector, call-centre operators.

www.ingramcontent.com/pod-product-compliance
Lightning Source LLC
LaVergne TN
LVHW081408110826
845149LV00010B/1671

* 9 7 8 9 2 6 4 4 6 6 4 7 0 *